THE VOYAGE
THE MATTHEW

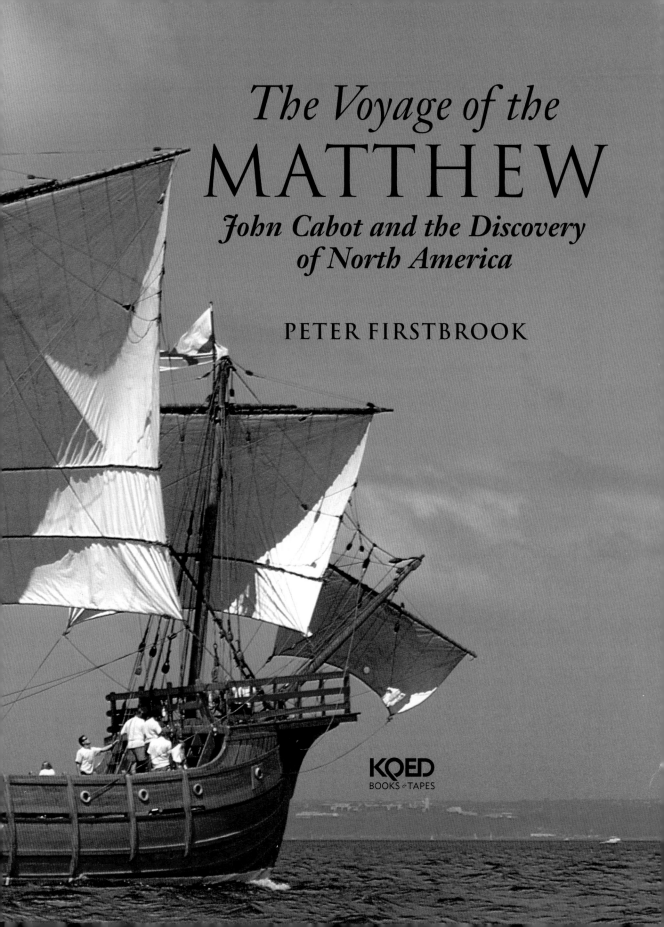

The Voyage of the
MATTHEW

John Cabot and the Discovery
of North America

PETER FIRSTBROOK

KQED
BOOKS & TAPES

Bay Books & Tapes, 555 De Haro Street, Suite 220, San Francisco, CA 94107.

KQED Books & Tapes is a Service Mark of KQED, Inc.

First published 1997 by BBC Books. This U.S. edition published 1997 by Bay Books & Tapes, by arrangement with BBC Books, a division of BBC Worldwide, Ltd.

Publisher: James Connolly
Editorial Director: Pamela Byers
Cover Design: Jeffrey O'Rourke
Picture Research: Frances Topp
Maps: Line and Line

Educational and nonprofit groups wishing to order this book at attractive quantity discounts may contact Bay Books & Tapes, Attn: Special Sales Dept., 555 De Haro Street, Suite 220, San Francisco, CA 94107.

Library of Congress Cataloguing-in-Publication Data

Firstbrook, P. L.
    The voyage of the Matthew : John Cabot and the discovery of
America / Peter Firstbrook ; foreword by H.R.H. Prince Phillip.
        p.   cm.
    Include bibliographical references and index.
    ISBN 0-912333-22-7
    1. Cabot, John, d. 1498? 2. Matthew (Ship) 3. America--Discovery
and exploration--British. 4. Firstbrook, P. L.--Journeys--America.
5. Explorers--England--Biography. 6. Explorers--America--Biography.
I. Title.
E129.C1F57 1997   97-11475
970.01'7--dc21   CIP

Manufactured in Hong Kong
10 9 8 7 6 5 4 3 2 1

Distributed to the trade by Publishers Group West

CONTENTS

ଡ଼ଡ଼ଡ଼ଡ଼ଡ଼ଡ଼

To the seamen of Europe the Atlantic has always been a challenge and a barrier. For none more so than those along the western seaboard from Spain to Norway. The Irish epic 'Navigatio Brendani' suggests that St. Brendan broke the barrier in the 6th century and the Norse Sagas relate that Leif Eriksson, the son of Erik the Red, established a small settlement on Newfoundland some 500 years later. There is also circumstantial evidence that fishermen from Bristol were fishing for cod on the Grand Banks off Newfoundland in the early 15th century.

Then in 1497 John Cabot set out from Bristol, under the patronage of King Henry VII, on one of the most remarkable voyages in the history of maritime discovery. The significance of the voyage of the 'Matthew' is that it took John Cabot to the mainland of North America and which eventually led to the migration of many English-speaking people to the countries of that continent.

The North Atlantic is not a comfortable environment at any time, and for the seamen of the 15th century in their small sailing ships it presented a formidable hazard. The chances of the 'Matthew' getting across and back were a great deal shorter than of the 'Apollo' reaching and returning from the moon. Even Columbus, five years earlier, could expect better weather conditions on his more southerly route.

This book sets Cabot's achievement in the greater context of the exciting and dynamic period of European maritime exploration. It also follows the fascinating story of the conception, design and construction of a replica of the 'Matthew'. No-one will follow the progress of the new 'Matthew' more closely than I as she marks the quincentenary of John Cabot's great adventure by following his track from Bristol to Newfoundland in May and June 1997.

I wish her Master and crew, God's speed and a safe passage.

ACKNOWLEDGEMENTS

My history master at school always kept a big sign over his blackboard with a quotation by Henry Ford. It said: *'History is Bunk'*. I now realize that Ford should have stuck with building cars, but despite my lack of attention during history classes I am not alone in recalling little about John Cabot. Christopher Columbus, Vasco da Gama, Bartholomew Diaz, Ferdinand Magellan and even John Cabot's own son Sebastian are all better known than Cabot himself, who seems somehow to have slipped unnoticed through a crack in the pieces that make up our mosaic of history. So it is appropriate, 500 years on from his great voyages, that John Cabot should now receive the credit he is due.

Inevitably, building a replica fifteenth-century ship, the production of a six-part television series and writing a book involve many dedicated and determined people, and I hope that those I am unable to mention here will accept my apologies. Our collective thanks should go first to St John Hartnell, chairman of the Cabot 500 Celebrations, who had the determination to see a new *Matthew* built, and to Mike Slade for generously underwriting the project. My thanks also to those who made the ship a reality: Peter Workman, director-general of the Cabot 500 Celebrations; David Redfern, their media co-ordinator and all the good-humoured and tolerant supporters in the office. On site, the project manager Mike Blackwell and the shipwrights gave us every assistance; they showed unlimited patience whenever I and my BBC colleagues wanted to film, even though our activities always interrupted theirs. Inevitably, we also made great demands on the skipper of the *Matthew*, David Alan-Williams; to him, his wife Laurel, Colin Mudie the designer, John Bremner, the crew, the sailmakers, the riggers and all those associated with the *Matthew*, can I say thank you for bringing alive a special piece of history?

My thanks also go to those who have worked with me at BBC Bristol. The television series would not have happened had it not been for the determination of my head of department, Jeremy Gibson, to get the programmes commissioned; throughout the production he has been a constant support. Making the series has been great fun, mainly because of the people involved. So my thanks also go to Peter Snow for presenting the programmes in his inimitable style, to director Steve Greenwood, to Liz Banks and Andrew Johnston for the research, to Judy Andrews, Liz Wilson and Jamie Merritt in the production office, and to Orlando Stuart, Eric Huyton and our other cameramen on the series.

At BBC Books, Sheila Ableman, Doug Young and Linda Blakemore guided me through the novel experience of writing a book.

Over the years I have come to realize that Henry Ford was profoundly wrong about history and I found both making the television series and writing this book an exiting and fulfilling experience. But I am, first and foremost, a filmmaker and not an historian. The book is presented primarily as a rattling good yarn and not as a profound historical work. It has no scholarly pretensions and the sources are secondary, so I have a special debt of gratitude to those on whose work I have drawn. A full bibliography is given at the back of the book, but a few deserve special mention: Dr James Williamson is generally regarded as the doyen of Cabotian history, and those who would like a fuller account of John Cabot should read his book, *The Cabot Voyages and Bristol Discovery under Henry VII*. Likewise, Professor David Quinn, Dr Alwyn Ruddock and Ian Wilson have written extensively on John Cabot and the Bristol fisherman. Dr John Kington at the Climatic Research Unit in Norwich was also a valuable source of advice.

My final thanks go to my family. They, of all people, have had to cope with the restless nights, piles of scattered books and my appropriation of the best computer in the house. My wife Paula has constantly reviewed various drafts and said all the right things at the right times. And my children – the best thing I can say to them is that at last I have time to come out to play.

Despite all the care and checking of the manuscript, my biggest worry is that mistakes and errors have still crept in. If so, it goes without saying that the responsibility is mine, but I trust they are neither so serious nor so glaring that they spoil what I hope you will find a fascinating story.

Peter Firstbrook
Truant, Bristol harbour

THE MOST IMPORTANT SHIP IN THE ENGLISH LANGUAGE

And all night long they sailed away;
And when the sun went down,
They whistled and warbled a moony song
To the echoing sound of a coppery gong,
In the shade of the mountains brown.

EDWARD LEAR, *The Jumblies*

Early in the morning of 24 June 1497 – Midsummer Day and, coincidentally, the feast of St John the Baptist – John Cabot stepped ashore on North American soil. Cabot became the first European of his age to land on the continent of North America and claim it for the English monarch, Henry VII. In doing so, he laid the foundation stone of English exploration and colonization. It is ironic that it should be an Italian who bears ultimate responsibility for North America becoming part of the English-speaking world, but, as a result of Cabot's endeavours, the *Matthew* can claim to be the most important ship in the English language.

Exactly where Cabot made his landing on that fateful morning in late June is uncertain – like so much else in his eventful life. It is most likely that the actual spot was near the northern tip of Newfoundland or across the straits in southern Labrador. Farther south in Newfoundland near Cape Bonavista is favoured by some, while others believe it may have been still farther south – in Nova Scotia or perhaps even Maine. But, however much else is uncertain about John Cabot and his life, that he made a landing in North America in June 1497 is undisputed fact.

'John Cabot' reads a medieval navigation instrument called an astrolabe,
which allowed mariners to calculate their position north or south of the equator.
The role of Cabot in the television series was played by the actor Guy Ransom.

Everyone knows that Christopher Columbus sailed across the Atlantic five years earlier in 1492 and that he can claim to have discovered the 'New World'. Yet, when Cabot made his historic landing in Newfoundland, Columbus and his crew were still exploring the Caribbean islands and no Spaniard landed on the North American continent proper until 1513. After four voyages across the Atlantic Columbus died in ignorance of the great land mass that lay just over the horizon to the north of his Caribbean islands, and until the end of his life he remained convinced that the land he had discovered was Marco Polo's Cathay.

John Cabot's Atlantic crossing of 1497 ranks as one of the greatest voyages of discovery of all time. But unlike Columbus who took the relatively gentle southerly trade-wind route to the West Indies with three ships, Cabot sailed across the North Atlantic against the prevailing winds and ocean currents with just one small three-masted caravel. Although shorter, this northern route was much harder on both ship and crew: in addition to unfavourable winds and currents, air and sea temperatures were cold even in June and, on approaching the North American continent, Cabot and his crew would have had to cope with dense fog over the Grand Banks and with the icebergs that drift south from Greenland's glaciers. Cabot's exploits cannot detract from the achievements of Columbus, who made his four remarkable trans-Atlantic voyages between 1492 and 1504. But Cabot's accomplishments are no less remarkable; had he returned from his last voyage in 1498 there is little doubt that he would have won himself a place in history equal to that of Columbus himself.

But it was not to be. On that final voyage Cabot and his fleet of ships disappeared. As a result, this great mariner has not received the credit he deserved. Columbus's son Fernando did much to secure his father's place in history by writing his biography. The one person who could have done this for Cabot was his son Sebastian. But one of Sebastian's great skills was self-promotion, and his father's biography was never written. Ironically, it is probably Sebastian who is better known, despite the fact that his father was undoubtedly the more accomplished mariner.

John Cabot's successful second voyage in 1497 is a major achievement in the history of man's exploration of his planet and a milestone along the road that led to the colonization of the world by Europeans. The journey is a fascinating story of skill, daring and good luck – one that combines the latest in contemporary understanding of the greater world beyond Europe with spying, political intrigue and the intense superpower rivalry of the day. Fortunately, sufficient information also survives about Cabot's final but unsuccessful voyage of 1498 to allow us to reconstruct what *might* have happened to the expedition, and this too is an almost unbelievable tale of exploration, survival and possibly even of murder.

◎◎◎◎◎◎◎

March 1996, and the new *Matthew* slipped quietly out of Bristol harbour and down the River Avon on the morning tide. In contrast to the fanfares and Victorian pageantry of the launch the previous September, the beginning of her sea trials was a quiet affair, but still the schoolchildren of Bristol turned out on the banks of the River Avon in their hundreds to see 'their' ship leave the city.

The weeks spent finishing the ship had been fraught, with the shipwrights working long into the night to get the vessel ready for sea. The *Matthew* had passed her safety inspections and all the navigation equipment was working, but much remained to be done and several shipwrights were still hard at work during that first sail, armed to the teeth with chisels and saws, desperately trying to make up lost time.

The ship was bound for Falmouth, and then on to London for a major promotional event. It seems that little had changed in five hundred years, for the owners of the new *Matthew* needed sponsorship just as much as John Cabot did for his voyages. Despite the delays and the tensions in building – which are typical for any project such as this – what had been achieved was remarkable. In two years an historic reconstruction had been built of a ship for which no plans or even a contemporary picture have survived. Yet now a real ship slipped down the muddy waters of the River Avon, bringing alive the historic past of one of England's great medieval maritime cities.

@@@@@@@@

Ironically, John Cabot would not have left that March morning – despite the fortuitous, bitterly cold east wind that took the modern replica swiftly down the Bristol Channel. The ship would not have worried him, for he would have marvelled at the fine finish that can be achieved with modern carbon-steel tools and would have envied the bronze bolts that hold the ship together and will never rust at sea.

What would have worried Cabot was the appearance of the comet *Hyakutake*. In March 1996 *Hyakutake* passed closer to earth than any other comet for decades and it could be seen clearly high in the night sky. Today, such a vision has everyone looking out in excited expectation, but few medieval sailors would have ventured to sea with such a threatening omen in the heavens. The maritime explorers of the late fifteenth century were setting off on voyages to unknown parts in the knowledge that some, perhaps many, would not return. Cabot was a skilled and well-travelled mariner and one of the leading cartographers of his day. But most of his crew were simple men, unable to read or write. They lived in a world whose forests were inhabited by hobgoblins and werewolves and where the waters of the uncharted oceans poured over its unknown limits in a roaring cascade. Comets were unwelcome apparitions at any time, and *Hyakutake*'s presence in the night sky would have been one uncertainty too many for Cabot's crew.

Above A chart of the Mediterranean and the North-east Atlantic, hand-drawn on vellum by Arraldus Domenech, 1486. This would be typical of the charts used by Cabot when he sailed from Spain to Bristol in 1494.
Opposite The Moon accompanies medieval sailors, from the fifteenth-century de Sphaera manuscript. The ships are three-masted carracks with well-developed aft-and forecastles.

Standing watch in the pitch dark at 3 a.m. on the forecastle of the *Matthew* brings home the reality of those early days of trans-oceanic exploration. Before Cabot's day a sea voyage consisted of little more than hopping from point to point on the coast, with the ship sailing from one known headland to another. But from about the middle of the fifteenth century there was a revolution in ocean voyaging. The Portuguese began their explorations south around Africa and, towards the end of the century, the Spanish struck across the Atlantic and discovered islands in the west. The sailors who set out on these voyages were now confident in the knowledge that they could find their way home again.

Yet few useful charts of the world's oceans had been drawn and most mariners were still sailing offshore with few navigational aids. There were no buoys or markers to help sailors avoid rocks and shoals, no weather forecasts to warn of gales, and no

The *Matthew* and the Royal Yacht *Britannia* together at Cowes Week
in August 1996. This was the first visit by the *Matthew* to Britain's premier
yachting event, and the last by *Britannia*. Members of the Royal Family took the
opportunity to pay an informal visit to the replica of Cabot's ship.

lifeboat service to assist when all seemed lost. In a world lit only by flame and where
the meagre light from a candle was extinguished early to save money, even the coastline would have been invisible on a cloudy or moonless night. These sailors must have
been highly skilled in the art of intuitive navigation to have survived – and even
thrived – on their perilous voyages. This is the excitement of such a project: the
Matthew is a piece of living and working history with the potential to help us learn
how the sailors of the fifteenth century handled their ships. For the crew of today's
Matthew it means going back to sailing school. They have to put behind them many
of the sailing techniques they have learnt over the years and develop new skills that
have been lost for centuries, for they must learn how to sail a ship that is effectively
500 years old.

❧❧❧❧❧❧❧

The trial sails in 1996 were a demanding time for the skipper of the new *Matthew*. David Allan-Williams is an experienced professional sailor and an accomplished yacht designer. He has competed in many of the top ocean races and was in the team that won the America's Cup for New Zealand; he has designed luxury sailing yachts and circumnavigated the world with Robin Knox-Johnston and Peter Blake in *Enza*, a state-of-the-art catamaran that beat the non-stop round-the-world record in 1994.

The constant needs of sponsorship made heavy demands on the *Matthew* and her crew throughout 1996. After the big public event at Canary Wharf in April, the ship returned to Bristol as the star attraction at the International Festival of the Sea at the end of May. This was the first time that a major international maritime festival had been held in Britain, and Bristol harbour was host to over 800 ships – the largest number of vessels it has held in its long history.

After the festival the *Matthew* left Bristol at the beginning of June bound for Ireland to continue her sailing trials, this time with prospective crew members on board. But tragedy struck: the *Matthew* was caught in an unseasonal gale in the Bristol Channel and Steve Blake, one of the shipwrights still working on board, fell and knocked his head and was seriously concussed. A search and rescue helicopter was called out and he was winched off and taken to hospital. Stevie eventually made a full recovery, but only after several months of convalescence. Later in the same voyage the pressurized hydraulic supply to the gearboxes developed a serious leak and the motorized propulsion units had to be shut down. The *Matthew*'s first visit to Ireland was eventually made at the end of the towrope of the Ballycotton lifeboat. Her inauspicious voyage was a timely reminder that in the late twentieth century the sea still holds surprises even for the most experienced sailors on board a well-prepared ship.

The *Matthew* was clearly in need of further work before she could safely continue her trials. Her ambitious sailing schedule was cut short and later that June she was taken to a shipyard in Falmouth for additional work before continuing to another big sailing festival in Brest and from there to the Isle of Wight for Cowes Week. In late August she was moved to the River Hamble in Southampton Water and taken out of the water for a comprehensive refit.

In December 1996 the *Matthew* made her final voyage of the year when she returned to her home port of Bristol for the winter. There was still much to do, but the lessons of 1996 had been learnt and changes had been made in preparation for the voyage across the unforgiving Atlantic Ocean the following year.

⊚⊚⊚⊚⊚⊚⊚⊚

CHAPTER 1

CABOT'S WORLD

TO MAKE AN AMBLONGUS PIE

Then, having prepared the paste, insert the whole carefully;
adding at the same time a small pigeon, 2 slices of beef,
4 cauliflowers, and any number of oysters.
Watch patiently 'till the crust begins to rise,
and add a pinch of salt from time to time.
Serve up in a clean dish, and throw the whole
out of the window as fast as possible.

EDWARD LEAR *Three recipes for Domestic Cookery*

The demand for spices which made unpalatable food more bearable brought about the great era of exploration at the end of the fifteenth century. Spices made bad meat at least reasonably edible as long as you did not look too closely at what you were eating. There had been an insatiable demand for these condiments ever since Marco Polo visited Cathay and opened up trading routes to the Far East. Great riches were made from trading in such luxury goods: spices were a mainstay, but fortunes were also made from silks, drugs, perfumes, precious stones, dyestuffs and carpets.

Between 1100 and 1300 goods from the Orient reached Europe either overland by caravan from China and central Asia or, more usually, across the Indian Ocean and through the Middle East. The overland journey took years to complete – if you survived the perils of robbery, illness and accident. The sea route was quicker though still hazardous, but if only one in every five ships with their profitable cargo survived the three-year passage the merchant-owner could sleep happy knowing that he

A map of the known world by the sixth-century traveller and
theologian Cosmas. He believed the world was a flat plane with the city of
Jerusalem in the centre. Beyond this lay the Garden of Eden irrigated by the
four Rivers of Paradise. Cosmas argued the sun was smaller than the earth
and revolved around a mountain to the north.

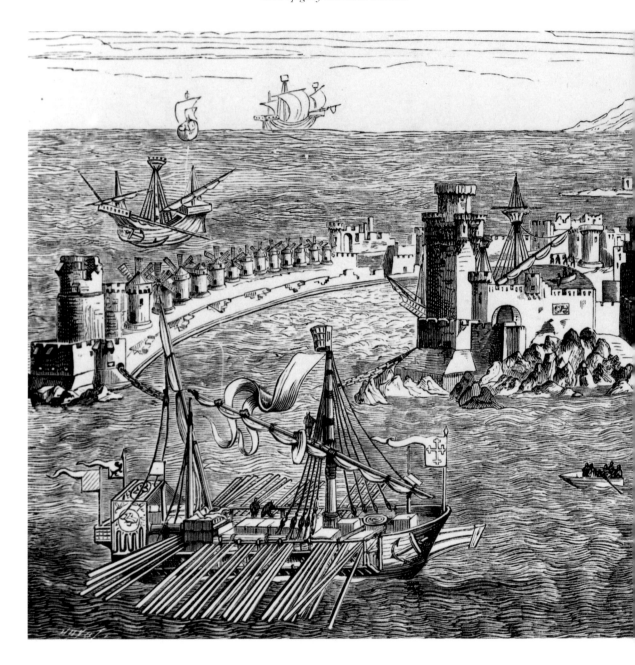

Rhodes harbour in 1483, when trade throughout the Mediterranean was still
dominated by Venice. The Mediterranean galley in the foreground is typical of the
period: the ship carries two masts supporting a square sail forward and a lateen sail aft.
The relatively poor sailing qualities of these ships meant that sail was often supplemented
by oars, usually manned by slaves. Judging by the position of the oars, the ship is probably
manoeuvring in harbour with the anchor ready to drop. These trading outposts were
always vulnerable to attack from both land and sea, and the heavily fortified positions
indicate how seriously the Venetians took the likelihood of an assault on the city.

would remain a rich man. Palms were greased at every stage of the journey and spices passed through at least a dozen hands before they were eventually sold on to the European customer. A sack of cinnamon, ginger, black pepper or nutmeg was worth a small fortune; fragrant ambergris, musk, attar of roses, silks, damasks, gold, Indian diamonds, Ceylonese pearls and, very probably, hallucinogenic drugs were all part of this lucrative trade with the Orient.

This all changed in 1453, when Constantinople – the greatest city in Christendom – fell before the relentless onslaught of the Ottoman Turks. To the Christians of Europe the Ottomans were the most ferocious of all barbarians. John Cabot lived for several years in both Venice and Genoa, and these Italian city-states had important trading colonies in the eastern Mediterranean, which were now overrun by the Turks. No doubt the news sent a shiver down many a dark Genoese alleyway; to young Cabot, who was only a toddler at the time, the significance of these events would not become obvious for another thirty-odd years. The fall of Constantinople cut off the supply of Oriental spices to Europe and the merchants were now desperate to find new routes to the Far East that would allow them to bypass the potentially hostile Islamic countries of the Middle East.

THE SPICE TRADE

The trade in exotic spices has been important for at least 4000 years and southern Arabia has always been a major trading centre for such luxuries. Arab traders tried to keep the true source of their goods secret and they spread bizarre tales about their origins; it was claimed that cassia was found in shallow lakes guarded by winged animals and that cinnamon grew in deep valleys infested by poisonous snakes. Most spices came by sea from the Moluccas or Spice Islands, and the Arabs were sailing to the Far East well before the Christian era.

By the tenth century Venice had profitable trading links with the Levant and, by the early thirteenth century, it had a monopoly of trade in the Middle East, making it a formidable power in Europe by the fifteenth century. Venetian merchants traded in Alexandria and sold their spices on to European buyer-distributors at exorbitant prices, protected by their monopoly.

By the middle of the fifteenth century other European traders knew the origin of the spices that reached Alexandria, but they could not break the Venetian monopoly. Competition to find a route to the spice-producing countries led eventually to the great voyages of discovery at the end of the fifteenth century, and it was the Portuguese who first suceeded in bringing spices from India to Europe around the Cape of Good Hope in 1501.

@@@@@@@@@

Two routes which bypassed Constantinople seemed to offer possibilities, although in 1453 neither had actually been attempted. One route was south around the tip of Africa, but the southward extent of the continent was still unknown and the prevailing opinion at the time was that the equatorial regions of the world were so hot and humid that human beings could not survive! The second route – westwards across the Atlantic Ocean – appeared to be no easier. If the world really was round, as many people now believed, then in theory it should be possible to sail west to find the East – Marco Polo's Cathay. It was to be another generation before either route was attempted, although the foundations for these voyages were already being laid in 1453. Ultimately, the stakes were even higher than just finding a new route to Asia, for the nation that controlled trade with the East would effectively dominate the known world.

While the good citizens of Genoa were fretting about the imminent arrival of blood-lusting Ottomans at their city gates, the people of Bristol had other worries on

22

A painting by the Renaissance artist Titian, showing Pope Alexander VI
presenting the papal legate Jacopo Pesaro to St Peter, c.1506. Alexander VI was
a notorious Borgia, and the most influential pope during Cabot's lifetime, as he was
responsible for dividing up the New World between Spain and Portugal. The Treaty of
Tordesillas stated that Portugal could claim everything east of a line drawn north-south
through the Atlantic, 370 leagues west of the Cape Verde Islands (approximately 40°W
on today's maps), and Spain everything to the west. This gave Spain rights to most
of the Americas and Portugal laid claim to Africa. The treaty also explains
why Brazilians still speak Portuguese today.

their plate (or, at least, in their glass) – they had run out of French wine. In 1453, after a long war of attrition in English-ruled Gascony, Bordeaux finally fell to the French and England lost her access to the vineyards of southern France. This hit Bristol particularly hard as there was a significant amount of trade between the city and Bordeaux. Before long the resourceful Bristol merchants were trading farther afield to Spain, Portugal, the Canary Islands and Madeira for wine, as well as sailing north to Iceland for cod to supply the endless demand in Roman Catholic England. As a result, Bristol was gaining a formidable reputation as a centre for experienced and skilled Atlantic sailors. As we shall find out later, it is even possible that Bristol fishermen might already have ventured even farther afield – across the Atlantic Ocean and into the previously unknown world.

☉☉☉☉☉☉☉☉

So young John Cabot grew up in a world where both the need and the opportunity for global exploration were just beginning. Until the early 1400s Europe had spent nearly a thousand years in limbo. After the last of the Roman legions was recalled in the fifth century the continent withdrew into itself. What little is known about the period that follows does not make pleasant reading. Intellectual life almost vanished from the continent and Europe descended into a period of constant warfare, lawlessness, corruption and an obsession with strange myths. Out of this anarchy rose the warrior aristocracies of Europe. The Church in Rome began to dominate the whole of Europe and, after the turn of the millennium, the newly established monarchies courted favour with the Holy See by leading crusades to the Holy Land. The Church became the wealthiest landowner on the continent and a dominant factor in everyone's life, from baptism to burial. The religious laws laid down by the Vatican were uncompromising: to eat meat during Lent became a capital offence and sacrilege meant imprisonment. Control was exercised by the Pope through his cardinals, prelates, monsignors, archbishops, bishops and village priests. This was the world into which John Cabot and 70 million other Europeans were born.

In Cabot's day Popes lived like emperors, claiming divine (and unlimited) authority. Throughout the fifteenth and sixteenth centuries the infamous Borgias sat on the papal throne, the wealthiest and most powerful men in the known world – and also the most corrupt. The most influential Pope in Cabot's lifetime was Alexander VI (1492–1503), who was responsible for carving up the discoveries in the New World between Spain and Portugal. The Borgia reputation was notorious, and Alexander more than lived up to his family name. During his time as Pope the scandalous Vatican parties became more debauched than ever. Little was left to the imagination of the guests arriving at the papal palace. Living statues of young men and women in erotic poses graced the entrance to the party; inside, women danced naked before the guests, who would strip and join the dancers on the floor. Servants kept a count of each man's orgasms, for His Holiness greatly admired virility. When everyone had collapsed exhausted from the night's excesses the Pope would walk among his guests awarding prizes for performance. After the Church's jubilee in 1500 pilgrims returned home with wild stories of Vatican orgies, poisoned pontiffs, homicidal cardinals and nuns working as prostitutes on the streets of the holy city.

With such leadership, it is not surprising that corruption became endemic throughout Europe. The church levied taxes on everyone and archbishops, bishops and even the lower clergy grew comfortable on the excesses. John Morton, who was Henry VII's archbishop for a time, accused the Abbot of St Albans of:

> simony, usury, embezzlement and living publicly and continuously with harlots and mistreses within the precinct of the monastery and without

and the nation's monks of leading:

> a life of lasciviousness … of defiling the holy places, even the very churches of God, by infamous intercourse with nuns[1]

Priests by the thousand found it difficult – if not impossible – to live up to their vows of celibacy, and their solutions to the predicament varied. It was not unknown for church priests to offer women absolution in return for hasty intercourse in the confessional box. More often, they would take a mistress – or two. Despite these ad hoc solutions, clerics in some parts of the country were found guilty of up to a quarter of all sexual crimes against women although they made up only 2% of the male population. Not surprisingly, public perception of the priesthood was not always what it should have been. But the Church still remained a dominant power through wealth and threat.

Literacy was another powerful tool that was used by the Church and aristocracy, at least until Johann Gutenberg's presses began to tip the balance. Libraries guarded their valuable hand-copied books and manuscripts closely; until the end of the fifteenth century nearly all education, as well as access to libraries, was controlled by the Church. The clergy and most of the gentry were literate, but literacy rates at other levels of society were universally low; only one in every two men and fewer than one in five women could read or write. Signed papers, bonds, wills and marriage licences give an indication of literacy rates by class and profession. Most merchants and innkeepers were literate, but fewer than one in five peasants or labourers could read or write. In the poorest working classes very few bricklayers, shepherds or thatchers had any literacy skills at all. These figures are for national languages and do not give the full story – fewer people still could read and write Latin, which was the language of the Church, of law and of government. So the vast majority of people were excluded from any involvement in the machinery of power.

As a master mariner John Cabot would have been able to read and to write, and he was also a skilled cartographer. Growing up in Genoa, he would have spoken the local dialect of Italian; later in life he probably acquired some Arabic and Spanish and, eventually, English, although there is no historical record of his linguistic abilities.

◎◎◎◎◎◎◎

When John Cabot arrived in Bristol in late 1494 or early 1495 the population of England was under three million. The biggest city was London, with 50,000 people; Bristol was second, with 10,000 inhabitants – barely the population of a modern small town. The majority of people – 80 to 90% of the population – lived in the countryside and worked outdoors in backbreaking labour from sunrise to sundown.

It is a picture of England that would barely be recognisable today, and a prosperous peasant lived in conditions that few of us could tolerate. His single-story cottage of thatch with wattle and mud walls was surrounded by a vegetable garden. The family shared their large, barn-like home with cattle, pigs, hens and hay for the

Life in a kitchen during the middle ages, from the Luttrell Psalter, 1430.
The quality and diversity of food varied greatly according to your wealth and status.
The wealthiest families were served huge meals with many courses every day;
meat was often salted and would be boiled up in huge copper vats.

winter. The living room was gloomy, the walls coated with soot, and the clay floor was covered with loose marsh reeds. A single large bedstead was used by all the family – children, parents and grandparents alike – and was shared with a menagerie of rats, lice, fleas and other vermin. These were the wealthier peasants; others were not so lucky. The poorest existed as best they could in tiny, basic hovels that lacked the most basic amenities.

People survived on the land and had little contact with their neighbours living in a similar tiny hamlet perhaps only 15 or 20 miles (25-30 kilometres) away. With the exception of pregnant women and very young children, everyone laboured in the fields throughout the daylight hours. Their agricultural tools were basic – forks, rakes, spades, scythes, picks and balanced sickles. There was little iron for ploughshares, and horses and oxen were a luxury few could afford. It was a hard, tough life.

People usually took two meals a day, the first after a morning's work at 10 a.m. and a second in the early evening before it got dark. Food was monotonous and often not very nourishing: pottage, vegetables, occasionally some meat, and dried fish during Lent and on any one of scores of other religious days during the year. Beer, however, was cheap and was drunk in vast quantities. In Henry VII's time the individual allowance was a gallon a day – even for young children. But famine brought hard times when peasants sometimes sold everything they possessed and resorted to eating roots, grass and even bark to survive. Before the Black Death in the fourteenth century famines were more common than in Cabot's day; cannibalism was not unknown and reports spread of people eating their own children to survive; strangers ran the risk of being waylaid and killed for food and even corpses hanging from the gallows might be torn down for food.

POTTAGE

This was the medieval stand-by for everyday meals. Often the broth was made with vegetables only, but it was based on bone stock and meat was added if the Church or your personal wealth allowed. Ingredients depended on what was available, but a typical pottage might include:[2]

> *2lb shin of beef (if meat-based)*
> *4–6 small pieces of marrow bone*
> *Parsnips, celery, leeks, onions,*
> *carrots, white cabbage*
> *White breadcrumbs*
> *½ gallon of water*
> *Available herbs*
> *Salt to taste*

The meat is cut into manageable cubes, brought to the boil and simmered for two to three hours. Vegetables are boiled whole or in large pieces for ten minutes; the marrow is removed from the bones and everything is added together. Excess fat should be skimmed off before serving.

@@@@@@@@@@

Not surprisingly, people in the Middle Ages were smaller than today. A typical man stood an inch or two over five feet (1.52 metres) and weighed 135 pounds (61 kilograms); women were shorter and lighter. Nor was life expectancy in the fifteenth century high. One in every six or seven children did not survive to celebrate its first birthday. Such was the uncertainty of life that, at any given time, half of all adults were widowed and actively looking for a new partner. If a man lived beyond 45 he was considered old; his hair would be grey and to us he would have looked twice his age. This tenuous hold on life was not restricted to peasants toiling in the fields. The wife of one Lord Mayor of London bore twenty children, none of whom survived childhood.

The scourges of the people were ignorance and disease. The main killers were pulmonary infections, dysentery, famine-sickness, typhus, tuberculosis, diphtheria, measles, smallpox and a variety of fevers that all took their toll in a seemingly endless procession; leprosy and rickets struck many of the survivors. But nothing prepared the population of Europe for the Black Death, which swept across the continent in the middle of the fourteenth century.

The Black Death, or more correctly bubonic plague, is caused by a bacillus that lives in the bloodstream of rats and is transmitted to humans by the flea. The plague was endemic in China and travelled across Central Asia to the Crimea and then to Europe, spreading like fire in a wood store. The Black Death arrived in England in 1348 and within two years had killed between one-third and one-half of the population. The consequences for the country were devastating. From a population of about 3.75 million in 1348 numbers dwindled to a little over 2 million by 1400, slowly recovering after about 1430 to no more than 3 million by the early sixteenth century.

@@@@@@@@

Life was more structured in the cities but was hardly more comfortable. When John Cabot arrived in Bristol, the city of 10,000 people was dominated by a large medieval castle surrounded by a defensive city wall, turrets and reinforced gates. Cabot would have come by sea, sailing the seven miles from the Bristol Channel up the River Avon, through the impressive gorge and into the very heart of the fortified city.

Here, ships from a dozen countries squatted on the mud for nine hours in every twelve, waiting for high water to lift them free again. Bristol survived on trade, and the merchants went to great lengths to protect their livelihood. Wheeled carts were banned from the harbour lest they damage the structure of the cellars below, and the goods waiting to be loaded into ships were dragged to the quayside on wooden sledges by young, very fit men. Down by the harbour the marshy land was low and liable to flooding, providing a perfect place for malaria-carrying mosquitoes to breed.

Away from the stink of the river the narrow, twisting streets wound up the hills on which the city is built. Land inside the city wall was valuable and nothing could be wasted: the narrowest passageways were barely the width of a man's shoulders.

Shops and houses opened directly on to the street. Sanitation was non-existent and the hilly streets ran with urine and excrement. Sunshine rarely reached the ground as each storey jutted out beyond the one below, four or five storeys high, where people could shake hands with their neighbour opposite through an open window.

When Cabot arrived in Bristol his first priority was to ingratiate himself with the merchants of Bristol, who were the wealthy owners of the ships that traded from the port. The wealthy merchants were infamous, living almost as a law unto themselves. Fabulously rich and powerful, these were men who even the king hesitated to cross. They lived well in large, timber-framed houses in their favoured residential area in Redcliffe Street. Here, away from the squalor of the rest of the city, they could look out across the river and check on the ships on which their wealth depended.

In many ways their houses were uncomfortable by today's standards – damp, cold and reeking from the inadequate sanitation. Yet in other ways living conditions were very attractive and spacious. Because these merchants imported luxuries like carpets and tapestries into the country they had access to some of the most fashionable and elegant furnishings of the day. You would enter their house through an impressive, strong door into a vestibule and from there go into the living room, dominated by a huge fireplace. The ceilings were elegantly timbered and the glazed windows would open. Off this room would have been a drawing room in which the merchants discussed their private deals and a parlour for family conversation and meals.

Mealtimes were important and contrasted strikingly with the meagre fare of rural peasants. An everyday meal for a man of standing could run to fifteen or twenty dishes. Often whole oxen would be eaten; these were preserved in salt and then boiled up in great copper vats. On special occasions a whole stag might be roasted in the great fireplace, and served up crisped and larded. Napkins were unknown and people wiped their fingers and blew their noses on their sleeves – or those of a passing servant. Food was eaten with one's fingers; clothes were filthy, and bodies too, even in the best households.

As an Italian, John Cabot would have been appalled at the manners and shear gluttony he encountered in England. Raimondo de Soncino, writing of Cabot's 1497

Overleaf Bristol around 1670 from a print by James Millerd showing a city which Cabot would still recognize. The confluence of the rivers Frome (top) and Avon (bottom) form a U-shape, in which the fortified part of the city was built. To the northwest is the cathedral. In the centre is Bristol bridge, immediately north of which is John Cabot's local church. St Nicholas still survives and is now a tourist information centre. St Nicholas Street, where Cabot rented a house, runs to the west and north from the church. Redcliffe Street runs along the southeast bank of the River Avon. Here the wealthy merchants of Bristol built grand houses from which they could keep watch over the unloading of their ships in the harbour. St Mary's, Redcliffe, is at the bottom of the map.

BISHOPS PARK

vervay to ý hot well
Water house
The Bishops Park
Eliz. Hospitall
The Gaunt
The Lower greene
The Colledge Greene
The Bishops Pallace
The Cathedrall
St. Austins

St. Austins Back
St. Steevens
ý Key head

Frog-lane
Trenchee-lane
White lodg
St Michaels hill
Prior st. Froome Bridg
Froome gate
Froome stu.

H
G
I
L
M
D
E
C
B
N
A

Cotne st.
High Street
St. Mary

Channons Marsh

The Arms of the See

The Key
Lamer stay.
The Tower
Tower st.

ý Woodkey

Froome flu.
Gibb

ý Boulding greene

The Marsh

St Mary
Labram st.
Marsh st.
King st.
Bank
St Mary gate
St Nicholas Back
St Nicholas Leane

Avon fluvius

ý gravenlng
Place

BRISTOLIA.

itur Urbs muris muros cingentibus altis
Foſos et foſsas unda prœterea replet
iterum cingunt virdantes gramina campi
Et sata quæ Cereris munere preſsa patent
replent pagi quæ rupibus horrida nulls.
Vel silvis nulla fœda palude virent
die duplicem ſedet Urbs celeberrima portum
Turrigerum tollens culmen in astra ſuum
idens binos super amnes æmula pontes
Fornicibus magnis flumina magna premens
hinc dant ventis roſtrata turgida puppes
Huc iterum plauſu Claſsis onuſta redit
Oriens merces merces Occaſus et Omnis
Et mare, per terras adehat Orbis, opes
ſit Emporium cui quis commercia callent.
Empturi properant undiq, turba virum
triaſq, ſuas redientis omnibus Urbis
Prœſtanti narrant non mediocre decus
taq, mirantes quibus haud ſatiantur ocelli
Briſtolia dicunt non reticendus honos
etenim celebres ſpatioſa fiddis amœna
Dulcis & inſignis priſca benigna, nitens
Deum Regem Regionem Crimina Pacem.
Servat adorat amat protegit Odit Habet.

Traine Mills
Reddiff backs
Reddiff gate
St Thomas Street
Tower st.

Reddiff Hill
St Mary Reddiff

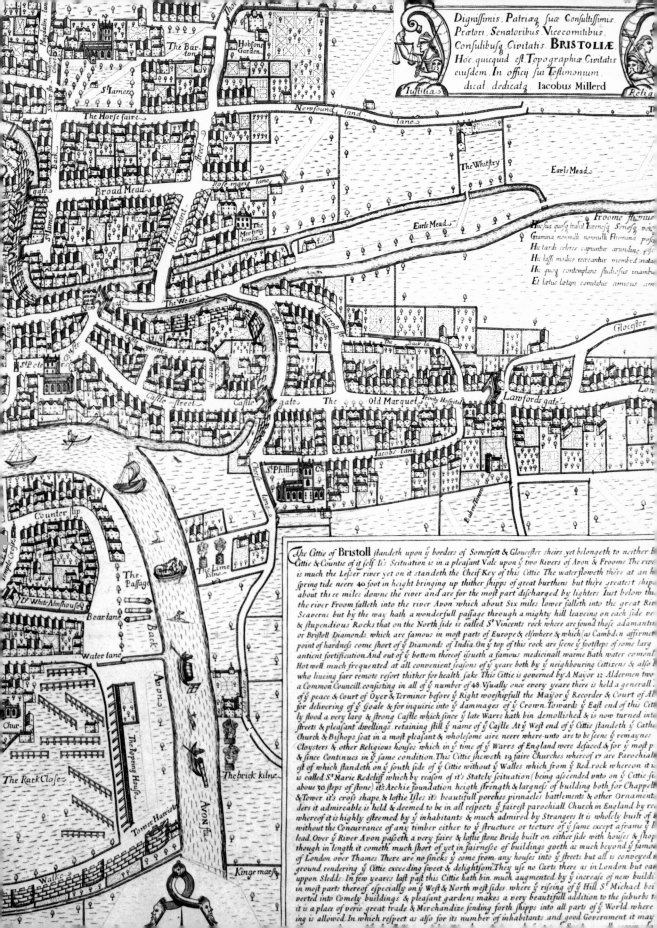

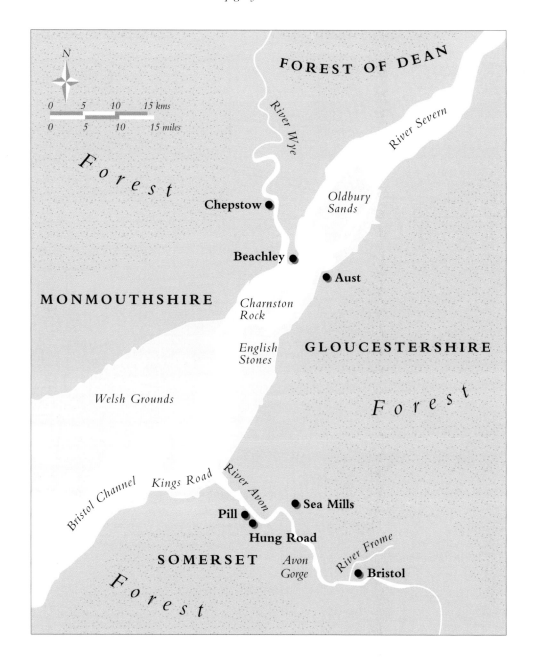

Bristol and the Severn Estuary. The confluence of the Frome and Avon provided a strategically defensible site for a Saxon settlement called *Brygstowe,* or 'place of the bridge'. The name became corrupted to *Brygstore* and then *Bristowe.* Situated seven miles (12km) up the River Avon, the high tidal range also gave the site an important strategic advantage. By the middle ages, the city's favourable western position allowed trade to flourish despite the hazardous approach up the Bristol Channel. Across the Severn Estuary, the forests of the Wye and Dean were probably used to supply the oak to build the *Matthew.* The timber would have been transported into the city on barges.

voyage to the Duke of Milan, felt obliged to finish his letter:

> Meanwhile I stay on in this country, eating ten or twelve courses at each meal, and spending three hours at table twice every day, for the love of your excellency, to whom I humbly commend myself...[3]

Bristol's wealth was founded on the importance of the port. Roads were generally in such a poor state that river navigation was essential for moving bulky goods such as grain and timber. Coastal transport was also crucial to the economy of the country and most regional trade was between the many harbours around the irregular coastline of the British Islands. From the North Sea and the Baltic came essentials such as fish, salt and timber and forest products such as pitch, tar and potash. Salt and wine were imported from the west coast of France. Trade with Mediterranean countries and beyond was mainly in imported luxuries, such as spices, drugs, perfumes, sugar, precious stones, dyestuffs (indigo, madder, saffron), alum and carpets. The outward-bound commodities were mainly woollens and linens, along with raw wool, metals and hides.

A MEDIEVAL FEAST

First Course
Brawn with sharp sauce, Boar's Head served with hot spiced gravy, Cygnets, Capon, Pheasant, Heron, Sturgeon with Pike sauce, baked Custard Tart with dried fruits, a sugar and paste centre-piece called a Soltette

Second Course
Venison stew with redcurrant jelly, Sucking Pig with forcemeat, Peacocks, Cranes, roast Venison, Rabbit, Bitterns, Chickens, fried Brawn with a tart vinegar sauce, another Soltette

Third Course
Dish of White Curd and White Meat with Almonds, Quince Pie, Egret, Curlew, Perch, Pigeons, Quail, Snipe, Lark Pie, Rabbit, Jellied Eggs, Fritters, Sweetmeats, Pastries, another Soltette

This was an exceptionally fine dinner,[4] although guests would not have been expected to eat all that was on offer for every course! The 'brawn' of the first course was a pudding eaten with the main dish, the boar's head – which was armed with its tusks and elaborately decorated.

@@@@@@@@@

In many ways the location of Bristol – several miles up a winding river, which itself is at the head of a long channel giving access to the open sea – was unusual. The Bristol Channel has the second highest tidal range in the world, with up to 50 feet (15 metres) between low and high water at spring tides. This huge range produces fast tidal currents, six knots or more being common – twice the normal speed of a heavily-laden medieval ship. The Channel is bordered on both sides by shallows, mud flats and outcrops of rock, and in Cabot's day there were no navigational marks offshore.

Yet Bristol also had its advantages: the strong tides allowed ships entering and leaving the harbour to drift with a favourable current if the wind was not blowing from the right direction. The big tidal range and narrow entrance through the gorge also served as important defences for the city when it was founded in the Dark Ages. The tide meant that attacking ships risked being left high and dry, making them vulnerable to attack from the shore. This protection, however, did not stop the city being ransacked more than once by the Vikings.

As England's main western port, Bristol flourished. Shortly after Cabot's voyage the city was remembered by one local merchant as:

> a noble towne of grete trate and many shippes … The shippes and botes comen into ij [each] partes of the towne, the one is called the backe and the other the keye …[5]

Bristol's seafarers had an excellent reputation. By the fifteenth century the knowledge of the local pilots was being included in the sailing guides of the time (called 'rutters') – and the dangers of the Bristol Channel were considerable. Even today's yachtsman, with modern navigational instruments, good charts, navigational marks and diesel engines, treats it with respect. In the past it has been called:

> a gulf with sands, islands and reefs, often swept by fierce and sudden north-westerly gales, chequered by furiously running tides and currents setting sometimes directly on to the places a ship should avoid, and a seaway of which the navigation has never been well known to foreign seamen …[6]

Near the mouth of the River Avon, about three miles from the town, was the anchorage of Hung Road, while in the Channel off Portishead was another anchorage called King Road. Here ships waited for the tide to carry them up into the river or for a favourable wind to take them down channel. Lighters, ships' boats and ferries sailed constantly between the two roads and the city port, as well as serving the many creeks and 'pills' along the River Avon and Severn Estuary. To take a boat down the river from Bristol to Hung Road cost one penny (1d) and to King Road it was 2d. River pilots – all of them skilled mariners appointed by the town council – brought ships into and out of the harbour.

It was important for the city to maintain a good reputation, especially as it depended so much on international trade, so the ordinances laid down to maintain the harbour and anchorages were precise. The pilots arranged where the ships were to be moored and the penalty for refusing to move when ordered was 100 ducats (the exchange rate was five shillings to the ducat), 80 ducats going to the Chamber of Bristol and 20 ducats to the bailiff or pilot presenting the case. Anchors could only be dropped with permission and no sand or ballast was to be dumped. The harbour was extensive and needed constant maintenance and repair. The banks at St Augustine's Back and around the edges of the marsh were made firm with stakes sunk into the mud and the gaps were filled with sticks, brushwood and rubble. In wintertime labourers were paid an extra 1d a day for working in the water in cold or frosty weather.

Owning a medieval ship was a high-risk business, but the profits could be enormous. Although an individual might own a ship outright it was customary for Bristol ships to be operated by partnerships or groups of shareholders. Group ownership spread the risk if a ship and her cargo were lost, but it added to the natural conservatism of ship design because several owners were more difficult to persuade than just one if a shipwright wanted to introduce innovations in a ship's design.

To the merchants of Bristol these ships were their livelihood and disaster could ruin their business. Unless carefully looked after any vessel is a potential shipwreck, and experienced masters like John Cabot made sure that everything on board was checked and tested before departure. The inside of the ship was scoured and doused with vinegar to subdue the stench from the journey just ended. Outside, the planking of the hull was checked and leaking seams were recaulked in preparation for the voyage to come. The city's merchants built and maintained their ships to the highest order partly, at least, to withstand the strains of drying out at low tide in the harbour; hence the expression 'Shipshape and Bristol fashion'.

@@@@@@@@

Until the end of the fifteenth century most ships sailed along the coast, hopping from one known point to another and rarely venturing far from shore. To the sailors of the medieval world the Atlantic Ocean beyond the horizon was known as the 'Sea of Darkness'. It was still a popular notion among some that the world was flat and that if you sailed too far you could fall off the edge. But by the fifteenth century more experienced sailors and cartographers had accepted that the world was indeed round. When Cabot left Bristol in 1497 it was quite clear in his mind that he was sailing west across the Atlantic to find Cathay, which previously had only been reached by going overland in an easterly direction.

The sailors of classical Greece were accustomed to seeing the tops of mountains becoming visible over the horizon before the land beneath appeared, and they were the first to realize that this must mean the Earth was round. The Greek philosopher Aristotle (who lived between 384 and 322BC) heard sailors talking of the phenomenon and wrote about its significance. He realized that the Earth was indeed round by observing an eclipse and deducing that only an orb could throw a circular shadow on the moon.

But Aristotle also made mistakes that had serious consequences more than a thousand years later. He knew of the existence of both the Indian subcontinent and the Iberian peninsula and, observing that land was heavier than water, he concluded that to be in balance the mass of each must be on opposite sides of the globe. He therefore argued that the distance between the two in a westerly direction across the Atlantic was not great and that there could be no land in between – effectively ruling out the existence of the continents of North and South America. Both Christopher Columbus and John Cabot made the same assumption when they sailed west across the Atlantic to find the fabled Orient. Aristotle's theory of the Earth formed the cornerstone of classical Greek geography, which divided the planet into five zones: two polar regions which were too cold to be inhabited, two temperate regions and a central equatorial zone. It was Roger Bacon and Albertus Magnus who later argued that because of its great heat the Equator would be incapable of sustaining life, and this theory persisted until the Portuguese crossed the Equator off Africa in 1471.

Eratosthenes, the Greek mathematician and astronomer, took the next major step in global geography in about 200BC when he calculated the Earth's circumference by measuring the difference in latitude between the cities of Syene (now Aswan) and Alexandria. He calculated that the Earth had a circumference of 252,000 stadia – a 'stadium' was the length of a running track at Olympia, probably 202 yards (184 metres). This equalled 25,137 modern nautical miles, making each degree equivalent to 69.83 nautical miles. The actual circumference is 21,600 nautical miles and a degree is exactly 60 nautical miles, so Eratosthenes was not too far out. The medieval Arab geographer Al-Farghani calculated a degree as 56.67 of an Arab mile, or 66.2 nautical miles, which was even closer.

But the work that probably had most influence on fifteenth-century explorers was that of Claudius Ptolemaeus, or Ptolemy, the astronomer, mathematician and geographer of the second century AD. His eight-volume treatise *Géographiké hyphégésis,* or 'Guide to Geography', was the standard reference on the subject until the discoveries of the fifteenth and sixteenth centuries showed that it was flawed. He inferred that Asia extended much farther east than it actually does, and this compounded the misunderstandings of early explorers like Columbus and Cabot. Ptolemy also underestimated the circumference of the earth by 30 per cent. Columbus used Ptolemy's information to argue that Cathay was much closer to Europe than it really was, so when he arrived in the Caribbean after covering more or less the expected distance he was convinced that he had landed on some of the many outlying islands of the Orient about which Marco Polo had written three centuries earlier.

The classical Greeks' understanding of the Earth was lost to Europe during the Dark Ages. In the sixth century the merchant-traveller and theologian Cosmas wrote the *Topographia Christiana,* which was based on the biblical account. Cosmas claimed that the world was a flat, rectangular plane surmounted by the sky, above which was Heaven (see illustration on page 18). In the middle of the map was Jerusalem, reflecting its position at the centre of the world. It was surrounded by ocean, beyond which was the Garden of Eden, irrigated by the four Rivers of Paradise. The sun, he maintained, was much smaller than the Earth and revolved around a conical mountain to the north. The Vatican accepted his theory, a decision that led to centuries of misunderstanding in the West about the shape of the Earth.

By the fifteenth century, however, the teachings of the classical Greeks had begun to influence medieval cartographers and it was generally accepted that the world was spherical, although the exact shape was the subject of considerable debate. Some believed the Earth to be a perfect sphere, others that it was a ball squashed at both ends, while yet others suggested that it might be pear-shaped. When it suited his purpose Columbus adopted the last argument.

This was the dawn of ocean travel and, as more information about the greater world accumulated, so the old ideas of what the world was like were constantly challenged. The Spanish colonized many of the Atlantic islands whilst the west coast of Africa was explored by the Portuguese. Bartholomew Diaz rounded the Cape of Good Hope in 1488 as part of a well-organized programme to find a route to India and the Spice Islands. In a constant search for information, sailors from these long trips were eagerly questioned about what they saw and found. There was also news of bizarre objects that had been found washed ashore: two bodies with Chinese-looking faces (probably Eskimos) were found on a beach in Flores in the Azores; bamboo thicker than any seen in Africa was picked up by Columbus's brother-in-law at Porto Santo in Madeira, along with a wooden carving; and, after westerly storms, a bean which grows in the Caribbean was often washed up along the western shores of Europe. It was called the sea bean, but later this was changed to *fava de Colón* (Columbus's bean) as people believed that it had provided Columbus with the inspiration to sail across the Atlantic in search of land.

As the fifteenth century drew to a close the time was ripe for major voyages of discovery. However, to meet the challenge required good ships, wealthy sponsors and pioneering mariners.

ⓔⓔⓔⓔⓔⓔⓔ

CHAPTER 2

THE ITALIAN CONNECTION

*Why did I leave my native land, to find
Sharp hailstones, snow, and most disgusting wind?*

EDWARD LEAR *Eclogue*

W hen John Cabot first arrived in Bristol sometime in late 1494 or early 1495 the medieval city was England's gateway to the Atlantic and the country's most prosperous seaport after London. Cabot was in his mid-forties, with a reputation as a skilled and experienced mariner. He had sailed throughout the Mediterranean and he is even thought to have travelled overland as far as Mecca (presumably disguised as a Muslim pilgrim). But the relatively calm and tideless waters of the Mediterranean had not prepared Cabot for what he was about to find in Bristol. The winding River Avon cuts through a gorge where near-vertical cliffs rise more than 300 feet (90 metres) above the waters below. At high tide the river is navigable beyond the city, but because of the 50-foot (15-metre) tidal range the channel becomes a deep chasm lying between glistening walls of wet mud at low water.

Quite what Cabot made of all this on his first visit is not known – and this is both the problem and the exciting challenge of documenting his life, for very little is recorded although much more can be deduced. Cabot's achievements have long been overshadowed by those of Christopher Columbus and other great maritime explorers of the late fifteenth and early sixteenth centuries. Part of the reason for this is that so many of the better known voyages are well documented. Diaries, letters, reports and maps give historians a huge resource from which to reconstruct these epic ventures.

'John Cabot' on the deck of the *Matthew,* from the BBC1 television series,
The Voyage of the Matthew. When he arrived in England in 1494–5, ocean navigation
was still in its infancy and John Cabot is reputed to have introduced maritime
charts into England from Italy and Spain.

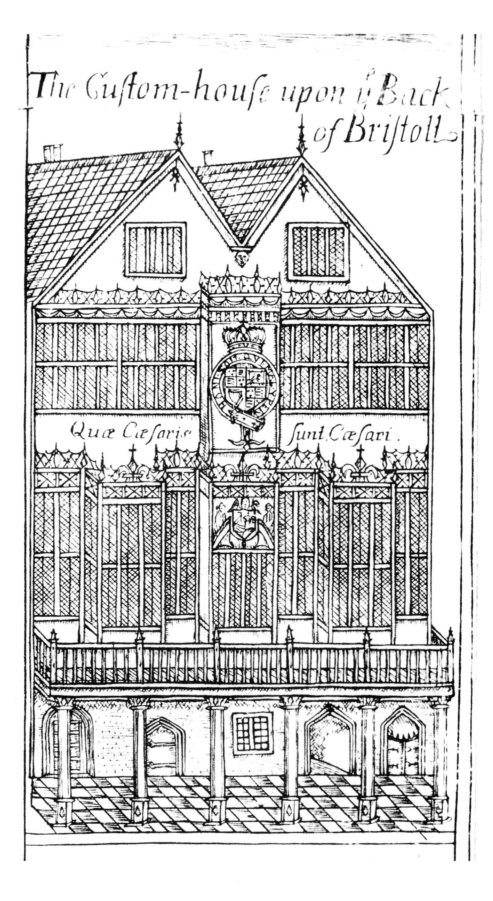

The Custom-house upon ẙ Back of Bristoll

Quæ Cæsaris sunt, Cæsari.

About John Cabot, by contrast, there is very little information that does not have to be qualified in some way. Had he survived his third and last Atlantic expedition in 1498 he would have returned a hero, perhaps more famous even than his contemporary Christopher Columbus. His life would have been recorded for posterity and his remarkable voyages better documented. Instead, we are left with very few facts from which to piece together the life of this resourceful and adventurous man whose achievements have never been fully acknowledged by history.

However, a small but valuable fistful of documentation has survived from which it is possible to reconstruct Cabot's life from these records (a chronology is given in Appendix 1). His family's rent book from St Nicholas Street in Bristol is held in the Record Office, Gloucester, letters patent from Henry VII granting royal authority for his voyages are in the vaults of the Public Record Office in London and details of his pension can be found in the muniments of Westminster Abbey.

Abroad, the civil archives in Milan and the Biblioteca Marciana in Venice hold reports of his voyages that were sent back by ambassadors in London; some of these are given in full in Appendix 2. In Spain can be found plans for harbour works in Valencia that were drawn up by Cabot in the early 1490s, and the National Archives at Simancas contain the most important record of all – a letter from an English spy called John Day (Appendix 2.6). Finally, in the Naval Museum in Madrid is a map dated 1500 that was drawn by a Spanish cartographer who was present on Columbus's voyages. This is the very first map of the world to show the outline of the North American continent. However, the Spanish did not land on the North American continent until 1513, so it is intriguing to speculate how they came by the information for the map – and the answer certainly involves Cabot's trans-Atlantic voyages.

These, plus a few civic records from Genoa and Venice, are the only papers about Cabot's activities that have so far come to light. Yet, even from these few enigmatic documents it is possible to piece together a reasonably comprehensive picture of the life of John Cabot.

@@@@@@@

Opposite The Customs House in Bristol, where revenues were collected by the city's customs collectors. Although taken from a seventeenth-century engraving by James Millerd, this timber-framed house is typical of the buildings in Cabot's Bristol.

Overleaf Cabot's Italy, from the atlas *Ptolemaeus Cosmographia Quanta Europa Tabula*. This chart was published in Ulm in Germany in 1482 by Leonardus Hol, and is an excellent example of an early woodcut map.

· Pannonie superior pars :~　　· Pannonie inferioris ps
½

.: Illiridis siue liburnie pars atq̃ dalmacie

repsa aplocus
Crepsa
insula
Curitautz
tulli
tiu cuciat

· SINVS · ADRIATICVS ·

gabi
Scardona insul
colensi

Insole diomede
y

Ancron
naualina
uia
balina
tursa
peda cupranio
tana
furnui
castru
asculum hadria
alpia
marina
tru
cen
em

cetrui
mursa
Sabina
poteri
diteini
bretua
Pinna ff
auia
maruruman
teana
ff

calfiou
Marsi
alsibui
rel
Praguu
interuni
nia
Vel
tunii
niu
Apenni
angulus
aurelianu
Petig
nu
mone
Ap
mus
ortona
fulmo

Equiculi
aena
amelia
amuic
bina
num
sepini
cesena uulturnus
Samnitz
cunai
aula
aufidena
Caro
auxanu
ru
ficuluni
Frenta
ni
bula
lucinum
ficrtun

tibur
praenet
mumentu
idem
nimuni
colonia
foat
alisa
telesia
beneuen
tus
arpe
Aquilouru
mucera uibar
apuloz ua

Larinu
lambui
uelani
losta
aunu
princer
num
ferea
li
rs
pinone
firua
ne foene
cales
suessa
teani
capua
trebuli
dusui
multurnu
pli
capu
ff
lacmus
ff
hriu
saig
arpe
Aquilouru

Campui
cafih
lium
lier
uni cume
mistenu
abella
neapolis
puce
nola
Apinesthe
Apuli lop
erdonia
siya
cumbria
ani
Iouii
uiare

ponta
Pandato
ria
Parthe
nope
pronta
iltha
Picentui
nuceria
suren
ti
numene pinone
Salernu
abellui
acula
satino
lium
Irpin
cranu
ne
uisia
biali
peucetu
sibpie
antibus ff

Pithecusa
Crupea
tampsa
ff
porcu
na ff
sauius
blanda
pestum
Lucanu
uche
aquilonia
Apenninus mons

strongile de
serta
birtenti
Magna gre
ca
metapon
tu
caruu
rum pudai
brendi
siu

laus
ff
Brucii
templa
ca
nimui
tru
turii
abitrum
laci
con
tu
cca
lacmiu p
penla
mo
Sinus Ta
rantinus
uerii
ipeuni
tuubara
ueteni
Calab
tchiru
Salen
tuu

diorine hicesia
phoericos
ericodes
liparia
Simul ispoin
asta
maria
Ienau
Sinus sci
lacius
ale
cium
tapia
nuni
ideunu
sull
sull

euonunos
uulcam
alui p̃m
torciun
ngin
locris
leuca petm
· ADRIATICVM ·

· SICILIE · INSVLE · PARS ·

84

88

83

82

81

80

39

Cabot was born in Italy around 1450, although the precise date and place are not certain. He first appears in written records held in Venice under his Italian name, Giovanni Caboto – 'caboto' being the Italian for a coasting seaman. A Senate entry dated 29 March 1476 confirms that Caboto was granted Venetian citizenship; since a precondition of this naturalization was that the individual had to be a resident of Venice for at least fifteen years, Caboto must have been living in the city by 1461 at the latest. Before that, it is likely that he was born and raised in Genoa. A contemporary living in London wrote of him in 1498: *'another Genoese like Columbus'*.[1] Caboto's own son, Sebastian, also claimed that his father was from Genoa.

There are records of a family with the name Caboto living in the small town of Gaëta in the kingdom of Naples. Their names disappear from the public records by 1443, so it is possible that the Caboto family moved from Gaëta to Genoa before Giovanni was born. Certainly, most historians now accept that Giovanni Caboto was born in Genoa in 1450 or 1451 – the same birthplace as Christopher Columbus and with no more than a year between them.

In the middle of the fifteenth century the republic of Genoa was one of the more prosperous of twenty-five principalities, states and kingdoms that eventually united to create modern Italy. Genoa itself was a small medieval walled city squeezed along the steep, rocky coastline of what is now the Italian Riviera. It probably had no more than 35,000 inhabitants at the time of Caboto's birth, although there might have been twice as many living outside the city walls. The city was built around a fine natural harbour, and even today it rivals Marseilles as the leading European port in the Mediterranean. Although the city was relatively wealthy in the fifteenth century, the Genoese built few grand buildings like their Roman or Venetian counterparts, and the passageways were so narrow that it was said that horsemen had to turn in their toes when riding through the streets of the old city.

The city's wealth was founded in the twelfth century when Genoa began to dominate the region, laying the foundations of her naval power and civic prosperity. The city profited from the crusades, during which Genoese ships transported Christian knights to the Middle East and returned laden with booty. The merchants grew wealthy on the newly-awakened European demand for goods from the Middle East and they established trading communities throughout the Mediterranean. Genoese forts and trading posts were set up as far east as the Aegean and eventually in the Black Sea. However, the city's trading activities, helped by friendly relations with the Byzantine Empire, brought it into increasing rivalry with Venice. This eventually broke out into open warfare in the mid-thirteenth century just as Genoese power reached its height. The city finally acknowledged Venetian supremacy in the war of 1378–81.

MARCO POLO

Marco Polo (1254?–1324) was a Venetian traveller and writer who provided Europeans with their first detailed report of life in the Far East. His father and uncle were merchants who, in 1260, travelled to China, returning to Venice in 1269. Two years later they went back to China, this time taking young Marco. They travelled from what is now Israel to the Persian Gulf, north through Iran, up the River Oxus and from there to Sinkiang Province in China; they finally crossed the Gobi Desert to the court of Kublai Khan at Shangdu, where they arrived in 1275. They were the first Europeans to visit these regions. Marco joined Kublai Khan's diplomatic service and for three years was governor of the Chinese city of Yangzhou.

The Polos left China in 1292 and returned by sea to Iran by way of Sumatra, the Indian Ocean and the Persian Gulf, then proceeded overland through north-western Iran and along the coast of the Black Sea, arriving back in Venice in 1295. In 1298 Polo was taken prisoner during a sea battle between Venice and Genoa, and it was during his imprisonment in Genoa that he dictated to a fellow prisoner a detailed account of his travels. He was released in 1299 and returned to Venice.

His book, *The Travels of Marco Polo* (which was first published in French), is probably the most famous and influential travel book ever written. Its vivid detail gave medieval Europeans their first knowledge of China and of other Asian countries including Thailand, Japan, Vietnam, Ceylon, Tibet, India and Burma. For a long time it was the only source of information on the geography and life of the Far East and it became the basis for some of the first accurate maps of Asia made in Europe. The book inspired European explorers to take an interest in the Orient, including Vasco da Gama, Christopher Columbus and John Cabot.

On his deathbed Polo was asked by sceptical friends to withdraw his extraordinary claims; he replied, *'I have not told you half of what I saw'*.

Thus, Giovanni Caboto was born into a thriving maritime community. The harbour in Genoa was the focal point of the city; the quays were packed with ships of every shape, size and nationality. Galleys with slaves shackled to their oars brought unworked gold from Africa to be turned into coins and leaf by Genoese technicians; stumpy carracks – the supertankers of the age – imported the grain that was essential for the city's survival; iron ore was imported for weapon-makers and armourers, vegetables and fruit from Corsica, cotton from Cyprus, wine from the Aegean and timber from northern Europe. In her day Genoa was a major commercial centre for the western Mediterranean and Caboto was born with trading in his blood.

In the early 1450s Genoa was facing an uncertain future. To the north there was little trade through the pass over the western Apennines and the city was constantly threatened by the usual menaces of medieval Europe: robber knights, forest bandits and brigands, feudal warlords, civil wars and rampaging armies. Then, in 1453, a new development shook the city. Constantinople (now Istanbul) fell to the Ottoman Turks.

Above A fifteenth-century engraving of Venice. This is how the city would have
looked when John Cabot lived there from around 1461 to 1490.

Previous pages Genoa in 1461 around the time that John Cabot and his family
moved to Venice. The city was Italy's busiest port and was surrounded by strong defences.
In the foreground, trading galleys are at anchor and inside the harbour are the larger
carracks. The lighthouse, Genoa's heraldic symbol that Cabot would have known as a
child, was replaced in the sixteenth century by a similar structure. A small city even
by medieval standards, trade north over the mountains was limited and the
Genoese relied on access to the rest of the world by sea.

Throughout Caboto's childhood the Turks continued their advance westward, sweeping through Greece into the very heart of Europe. The whole of Christendom was shrinking in the face of the Ottomans, who were considered to be the most ferocious of all barbarians. The wealthy trading outposts of Genoa and Venice in the eastern Mediterranean fell under their relentless onslaught. Genoese merchants had grown wealthy from supplying the crusaders, and now their trade with the east was being strangled.

Watchtowers and battlements were built around the city overlooking the sea to the south, however, the most immediate threat came not from the Turks but from much nearer home – Spain. The kingdom of Aragon, which controlled most of the western Mediterranean including eastern Spain, Sardinia, Sicily and the southern half of Italy, dominated Genoa's access south to the rest of the world. Genoese ships fought their way out and then fought their way homewards again. Squeezed between France to the west and the Duchy of Milan to the east, this tiny city-state was invariably under the protection of one and equally inevitably at war with the other.

Despite these problems, Genoa continued to trade profitably. *'Genuensis ergo mercator'* ran the medieval Latin proverb: 'A Genoese, therefore a trader'. On the front page of a business ledger it was usual to enter the legend 'In the name of God and Profit'. The citizens were known for their crassness and materialism; even the poet Dante wrote of 'Genoa the shameless'. Unlike the corporate-minded Venetians, the Genoese trusted no-one and operated more as individuals within a small network of family or business partners. So secretive were they that merchants would even refuse to state the destination of their goods.

This was the world into which the young Giovanni Caboto was born. Certainly raised a Catholic, it is likely that he grew up with a sense of the uncertainty and insecurity of the world around him.

☺☺☺☺☺☺☺☺

By 1461, when Giovanni was ten or eleven, the Caboto family had moved to Venice, where they eventually became full citizens. Why they chose to move from Genoa to Venice is not known. The Venetians were certainly successful – like Genoa, the city had supplied the crusaders and developed trade with Asia. Venice had also acquired territory in regional wars and by the middle of the fifteenth century was the leading maritime power in the Christian world. It was this wealth of the great north Italian cities such as Venice that financed the great cultural achievements of the Renaissance, creating many fine works of art and architecture, new ideas and new opportunities. The beginning of the Turkish invasions in the 1450s and 1460s marked the end of Venetian greatness and her power began to fade as maritime supremacy passed to the

Portuguese; but, on the whole, life was still pretty good for the citizens of Venice when the Caboto family moved there in about 1461.

The Italian Renaissance also brought more prosaic achievements. Italian merchants and bankers developed commercial and financial techniques such as book-keeping and bills of exchange, and they now dominated commerce and finance across Europe. Because of this emphasis on record-keeping, details of Caboto's life in Venice now become more historically factual and we know that he was engaged in a variety of enterprises. Between 1482 and 1484 he bought and sold land in Venice: at least ten transactions are documented over a two-year period during which he traded in houses, meadowland and saltworks.

The title deeds from these transactions give us useful background to his family. One document refers to him as the son of the late Egidius, suggesting that Caboto's father had also moved to Venice (presumably from Genoa) and had died sometime before September 1482; another refers to a brother called Piero. In January 1484 Caboto borrowed 75 ducats from his wife's dowry; in return he signed over to her the rights to his personal property, including a house, a stretch of meadowland and three saltworks. These transactions suggest that he was married in the early 1480s to a woman called Mattea, which is the feminine version of the name Matteo, or Matthew. It might be that he later named his ship after his wife.

Documents for another property transaction in December 1484 refer to the fact that he was 'as father of a family of sons'; we know from other records that he had three sons, the middle one being Sebastian, who features in Caboto's later life and who was probably born in or before 1484. These documents do not rule out the possibility that he also had daughters, who would not necessarily have been mentioned in legal papers.

The property transactions suggest that his Genoese blood ran strong in his veins and that Giovanni Caboto was an experienced and canny merchant-trader.

Between 1485 and 1490, when he was in his mid- to late thirties, Caboto travelled extensively as an agent for a Venetian mercantile firm. Since the fall of Constantinople in 1453 Venetian merchants had been preoccupied with finding a new route to the Orient and re-establishing the spice trade with the East. At first the merchants looked east to find a new overland route, and this took Caboto on extensive travels to the Middle East. According to a report by Milan's ambassador to the court of King Henry VII of England, he travelled to the ports of the Black Sea as well as to the eastern Mediterranean. He went several times to Alexandria, an important spice market and the major port in Egypt, and as far south as Mecca. This was an adventurous and dangerous journey for a Christian to make – even if disguised as a Muslim pilgrim. Mecca was Islam's holiest shrine, on the caravan route from southwestern Arabia and a centre for the exchange of goods between east and west. As a merchant's agent, Caboto was searching for the source of spices and other oriental goods which were shipped from the East across the Indian Ocean in Arab dhows.

It was during these travels that Caboto came into contact with Arab traders, who would have spoken to him about the origin of their goods. It is likely that from such contacts the Venetian agent developed a keen sense of geography. We now know that these spices came mainly from the 'Spice Islands' of Indonesia – the Moluccas – which lie south of the Philippines. In Cabot's time European understanding of the geography of the Orient was hazy, being based mainly on the writings of Marco Polo. He learnt that the spices came from a land far to the East, and it may be that he began to wonder whether – if the world was indeed round – these places could be reached by sailing west.

Caboto was now in his late thirties, an experienced sailor and seasoned traveller, described by a contemporary as one 'who is a very good mariner, and has good skill in discovering new islands'.[2] He was used to long voyages by land and sea and, unlike most people in Europe, who travelled little, he was being exposed to a wide range of new ideas and to people who had journeyed even more widely than himself. This must have fired his imagination and it seems likely that it was during this time that Caboto became convinced, quite independently of Columbus's plans, that the shortest route to the Orient was westwards – across the Atlantic.

☺☺☺☺☺☺☺☺

Exactly when Giovanni and Mattea Caboto left Venice for Spain is unclear, although it is known that by 1490 the family had settled in Valencia on the Mediterranean coast. Caboto may well have been hopeful about the chances of finding a route westwards across the Atlantic to Cathay and Cipango (Japan) and realized that his chances of finding financial support for such a venture would be greater if he moved to the Iberian peninsula, closer to the Atlantic. Whatever his reasons, it must have been a big wrench to move to a foreign country, speaking a different language and with three sons – Ludovico, Sebastian and Sancio – all under the age of ten. It seems certain that Caboto left Venice around this time as there is no further record of him living there and local records in Valencia dated September 1492 (the same year that Columbus made his first voyage to the West Indies) state that:

> … we have been informed by Johan Cabot Montecalunya, the Venetian, that he arrived at the city two years ago, and during this time he has considered whether on the beach of this city a port could be constructed.[3]

51

We cannot be absolutely certain that Johan Cabot and Giovanni Caboto were one and the same, but historians now accept that Cabot had indeed moved to Valencia. Johan Cabot (the origin of the name Montecalunya is not known and was later dropped) is said to have designed and painted plans for a new port and offered to supervise construction of the new harbour. He had two meetings with the Spanish king and in February 1493 the work was approved. Unfortunately for Cabot, the decision was reversed a month later because of lack of funds and his job as a consultant effectively ended.

In that very same month Christopher Columbus returned from his first voyage to the Caribbean (although he was convinced that he had landed in Asia). On arrival, he set off overland to Seville in southern Spain to make his report to King Ferdinand and Queen Isabella, who had funded the expedition. Inconveniently, the king and queen had made one of their occasional moves of the royal court to Barcelona on the northeast coast. So Columbus set off once more, this time on the 700-mile (1100-kilometre) journey across Spain. He reached Barcelona in mid-April, passing on the way through towns and villages where people turned out in their thousands to admire his prizes from the New World. Columbus had with him exotic proof of his voyage: four surviving 'Indians', live parrots in cages, the skin of a giant iguana, spears tipped with fish bones, bundles of wool 'that grew on trees', spices, plants and dyes previously unknown to Europeans, treasure chests containing gold, a mask of hammered gold, bracelets, nose decorations and purses of gold dust.

This is where we come across one of those intriguing coincidences in history. On the way from Seville to Barcelona, Columbus and his entourage passed through Valencia, where John Cabot had only weeks before received news that his plans for a new harbour had failed. There is no record that the two men ever met, but as most of Spain seemed to be out on the streets gawking at the trophies from the Indies it is inconceivable that this extraordinary exhibition would have escaped Cabot's attention.

It is likely that the men did spend time together and shared their tales as sailors do the world over. Of the two, Cabot was the more experienced mariner despite Columbus's recent achievements. Cabot had seen the merchandise imported from Cathay and Cipango and other parts of Asia by Arab traders and he was also familiar with Marco Polo's work. The spices and plants that Columbus brought back were different from those that Cabot had seen in the markets of Arabia, and the naked Caribbean Indians in the entourage looked and behaved very differently from the Orientals he had met in the Middle East. If Columbus had indeed sailed to imperial China, where were the great trading ships, the harbours, the grand walled cities and the fabled wealth of Cathay? Cabot's experienced eye would not have been convinced by the display Columbus had brought from the Caribbean. He would have been sceptical of Columbus's claims, concluding that the Genoese explorer had not sailed far enough west across the ocean to have arrived in Cathay or Cipango.

This is, of course, supposition based on circumstantial coincidence. But around this time Cabot made the decision to seek funding for his own expedition to Asia and he visited the kings of both Spain and Portugal to persuade them to back the venture. But the Spanish royal couple had already funded Columbus and were celebrating his great success – so they were unlikely to finance a rival venture. As for the Portuguese, they had their sights firmly set on sailing around Africa to find a route to India, so they too showed little enthusiasm for Cabot's proposition.

So John Cabot and his young family packed their bags again and made their way to England; if Spain and Portugal were not interested, then his best chance of a royal benefactor was the king of England. The final inspiration for Cabot to search for Cathay across the Atlantic might well have come from Columbus's partial success in finding land in what we now know as the Caribbean.

Despite their common Genoese ancestry, Christopher Columbus and John Cabot were very different men and each was driven by different ambitions. Columbus was a mystic and combined Christian missionary enthusiasm with a zeal for the expansion of the Spanish empire and the profits of trade. With Cabot we hear nothing of religious fervour, although he would certainly have been raised a Catholic. In contrast to his contemporary, his single-minded ambition was to find a trading route to the riches of the Orient. In that respect he was a true son of Genoa.

So it was that John Cabot, born Giovanni Caboto in Genoa, sometime resident of Venice, a seasoned traveller in the Mediterranean and the Middle East and would-be civil engineer in Spain, found himself standing on the banks of the River Avon in Bristol planning a crossing of the Atlantic. Nothing in his eventful life would have prepared him for the strong tidal currents and huge tidal range of the Bristol Channel, the vast expanse of mud exposed at low water in the Avon or the harsh, rocky coastlines of the West Country and South Wales, all of which had to be confronted before a voyage across the ocean could begin.

After Cabot returned from his successful trans-Atlantic crossing in 1497, Lorenzo Pasqualigo wrote from London on 23 August to his brothers in Venice:

> The king here is much pleased at this; and he [Cabot] says that the tides are slack and do not run as they do here.[4]

How true.

❦❦❦❦❦❦❦❦

A. SALIZ / C. MUDIE

CHAPTER 3

DESIGNING CABOT'S CARAVEL

They went to sea in a sieve, they did;
In a sieve they went to sea:
In spite of all their friends could say,
On a winter's morn, on a stormy day,
In a sieve they went to sea.

EDWARD LEAR *The Jumblies*

The sailing ship, along with cathedrals and castles was the most complex piece of construction of pre-industrial times. For thousands of years, the ship combined technical complexity with versatility in a way that was not matched until the development of the steam engine. Sailing ships were the top technologies of their time and were built by the best engineers of the age to meet the needs of commerce or war. By the time the original *Matthew* was built in the 1490s even quite modest ships of the period had become complex pieces of machinery. Thousands of pieces of timber and hundreds of feet of rope were combined in such a way that the final structure could withstand the stresses and strains of a couple of decades of hard work. Even today, building a full-scale replica of John Cabot's boat was a complex exercise.

Colin Mudie's three-dimensional image of the *Matthew* as a three-masted caravel clearly shows his preferred sail-plan. The foremost sail is the spritsail, set on the sprit or bowsprit projecting in front of the vessel. Next is the foresail set on the foremast: this sail is shown with its bonnet – an extra panel laced on to increase the sail area. The biggest sail is the mainsail, set on the mainmast, and is shown with both bonnets rigged. The small triangular sail set aft is the lateen-rigged mizzen sail, modelled on the lateen sails carried on Arab dhows. Not shown is the main topsail, a small square sail set above the crow's nest. This tiny sail became known on board as the Noddy, because it was the one sail that was sometimes forgotten to be taken in before the engine was turned on to motor.

Marine historians build up an impression of these old vessels from three main sources: written accounts, contemporary pictures and archaeological wrecks. For the *Matthew*, however, there is no contemporary picture and, remarkably, no wreck of a fifteenth-century caravel has yet been found. All that could be learnt about the ship was culled from a few skimpy references in diaries and reports. So how was it possible to design and build a boat like this with such little information?

Colin Mudie, one of Britain's most celebrated yacht designers, was approached to design a replica of the *Matthew*. Mudie has vast experience of designing everything from small sailing boats to huge motor yachts, and he was the obvious choice for the commission because of his experience in designing a wide variety of other replica sailing craft or – as he prefers to call them – reconstructions. Previous such commissions undertaken by Mudie include a Greek trireme, a Viking longboat and a small open boat, the *Brendan* which was based on the vessel that St Brendan is reputed to have sailed across the Atlantic in the sixth century. Mudie's brief was to design a faithful copy of the *Matthew* that could sail swiftly and safely across the inhospitable North Atlantic.

Despite the lack of plans or pictures of the original, it was still possible to define quite closely what the *Matthew* was like. The evolution of ocean-going ships is a slow and logical process. Instinctively, shipbuilders over the ages have been cautious, conservative people as any mistakes in the design of ships are always serious for both crews and shipowners. It is therefore possible to trace the origins of the fifteenth-century caravel back to the beginning of the new millennium and before, when ocean travel was dominated by the Viking longship. This vessel had a narrow hull, usually symmetrical fore and aft, and carried a single mast and a simple spread of sail. The Norse were great maritime traders and warriors who travelled all along the North European coastline, up rivers to Russia and west to Iceland, Greenland and, eventually, North America. The Norse sagas written about these exploits often referred to cargo-carrying vessels called 'knarrs', but reliable evidence of what these ships looked like and how they were constructed was not found until the discovery in the 1960s of five Norse boats dating back to the tenth century.

Throughout the ninth and tenth centuries Norse raiding parties attacked cities and towns the length and breadth of Northern Europe; in France alone, the Vikings sacked Rouen and Paris on the Seine, Nantes and Tours on the Loire and Orléans and

A Viking longboat (the Osberg ship) showing the classic shape: a sweeping stem and stern with a clinker-built hull. With 'clinker' construction, planks overlap each other and the hull is well-braced internally with frames and cross beams. The hull has a shallow draft which allowed these ships to sail far up rivers and penetrate deep into Europe during raids. The ship carries a narrow, side-hung rudder and a single mast with a square sail.

Bordeaux on the Garonne. The invaders usually built fortified positions at the mouths of the rivers, and in time these defensive sites became permanent.

In AD911 a large company of Vikings (who the French called *Normands*) accepted territory in the lower Seine valley, which became known as Normandy. Little more than a century later the *Normands* were building a new invasion fleet, this time with their eyes fixed firmly on England. The full story of their preparations can be found in the most famous embroidery in the world – the Bayeux Tapestry. This medieval strip cartoon gives a detailed account of the preparation of the boats for the invasion and their passage across the English Channel.

Information on the development of ships over the next three or four hundred years comes from a range of diverse sources. Contemporary paintings always provide valuable clues, but a surprising amount of detail is to be found on city and port seals. Boats have appeared on clay tablets as far back as the Uruk period in Mesopotamia in the fourth millennium BC, but seals only became relatively common in Europe shortly after the Bayeux Tapestry was produced. These show a good, representative trend of ship design over several hundred years and give detail not available from literary sources. One of the problems with seals is that their round shape placed limitations on the artist, and in the past many of the features depicted have been dismissed as 'artistic licence'. But as more medieval wrecks have been discovered they have provided confirmation that many of the features shown on seals are accurate.

From the late eleventh century the simple Norse/Norman longboat evolved and developed into something much bigger and stronger. This brontosaurus of a ship is the mysterious 'hulk' and, as trade increased in Europe, it became an important carrier of cargo between England and the continent. Little is known about the hulk and no wreck has ever been found, but what little pictorial evidence survives suggests a vessel with a rounded, banana-shaped hull and a single mast. An excellent representation of a hulk can be found on the side of the font in Winchester Cathedral – and this is also the very earliest image of a ship with a stern rudder.

THE BAYEUX TAPESTRY

This medieval embroidery gives a detailed and informative account of the invasion of England by William of Normandy in 1066 and is remarkable both as a work of art and as an important historical source. The linen cloth measures 231 feet (70 metres) long by 19.5 inches (49.5 centimetres) wide and it has turned light brown with age. There are 72 embroidered scenes representing the Norman Conquest; eight colours are used and 1512 individual people can be identified.

The story begins with a prelude to Harold's visit to Bosham, near Chichester, on his way to Normandy (probably in 1064) and ends with the flight of Harold's English forces from Hastings in October 1066. The tapestry has decorative borders with figures of animals, scenes from the fables of Aesop and Phaedrus and others scenes relating to the main pictorial narrative. The embroidery has been restored more than once and some details of the restorations are of doubtful authenticity.

☺☺☺☺☺☺☺☺☺☺

Two scenes from the Bayeux Tapestry. *Above* Having cut down trees with straight-bladed axes, the Norman boat builders prepare the timbers. On the left, a workman uses the fork in a tree to support a plank, which he is working with a T-shaped smoothing axe. Other men are using smoothing axes, hammers and breast-augers for drilling holes. The striped hulls indicate the boats were clinker-built like the Viking longboats. In the foreground two shipwrights have beards, suggesting that older and more experienced craftsmen were involved in the final stages of construction. *Below* William the Conqueror approaches England. The long, narrow rudder used by the Vikings is inefficient at slow speeds, so the Normans improved its effectiveness by increasing the area at the bottom of the blade, where the water flow is least disturbed. The soldiers have increased the freeboard of the ship by using their shields to prevent water coming aboard. The helmsman aft and the crewman forward are sitting higher than the others on raised sections which evolved into the fore- and aftcastles. The helmsman has gathered in the sail, possibly to reduce the area to slow down or to maintain control of the ship.

PORT SEALS

A seal was an important emblem of a city's independence, and in England they date from around 1200 when many towns first received their charters. The seal of Exeter – one of the earliest – has been dated at around 1180. These miniatures were usually produced with great skill and care as the craft of engraving was well developed at this time; often they were made by the local goldsmiths, who were capable of the fine, precision work that was required. New miniatures were produced when the seal needed replacing, and maritime cities often depicted the latest in ship design as a matter of civic pride and so included recent innovations. Seals are preserved from ports on the Baltic and North Sea, the English Channel and the western coast of France.

Port seals from the late twelfth century onwards confirm the evolution of the European ship.
Above left The Winchelsea seal from the early 1300s shows the classic 'banana' shape of the
European hulk and most significantly, castellated structures at the bow and stern, giving archers
the advantage of height. These 'castles' are clearly free-standing structures on stilt-like legs,
which added both weight and windage and must have significantly decreased sailing performance.
The seal still shows a side-hung rudder and a clinker-hull. The engraving even highlights the
iron nails in the planking, and internal cross beams which protrude through the hull.
The star and moon suggests a night departure, as two crew members haul in the anchor
rope and another climbs the rigging, perhaps to set the sail.
Above right The seal of Kiel from the thirteenth century depicts the usual features of
a cog; a straight stem and a flat-bottomed hull produced a large-volume cargo ship.
The cog still retains the clinker-hull and single mast of its predecessors, but this ship now
has a centreline stern rudder and is very much bigger than the Viking and Norman ships.

ⓔⓔⓔⓔⓔⓔⓔⓔⓔⓔ

The stone font in Winchester Cathedral shows the round-bottomed
banana-shaped hull of a medieval hulk, but is built with 'reversed clinker', where
the planks overlap with the edges facing up rather than down. The font is dated
*c.*AD1170 and is the earliest known image of a European ship with a stern rudder.

Meanwhile on the continent, the Hanseatic League was developing a different
kind of cargo-carrier called a cog, which differs from the Norman longboats and the
hulk in having straight, raked (slanted) stem- and sternposts and a flat bottom, which
made it a capacious trading vessel. Like the hulk, the cog acquired a stern rudder
to replace the steering oar, but it still retained the single square sail and clinker
construction of the Norse ships ('clinker' refers to a hull that is constructed with
each plank overlapping the one below as in the Viking longboat on page 57). By its
evolutionary peak in the thirteenth century this big boat with a little name had
grown into a sea-going vessel of several hundred tons in its largest form and was
regarded as the archetypal ship of the high Middle Ages and the mainstay of the
Hanseatic League.

Until the late thirteenth century ships in northern Europe and the Mediterranean evolved along separate paths. But around the turn of the century the two
seafaring technologies began to merge. In Europe the cog, with its high clinker sides
and distinctively angled stem- and sternposts, was the main bulk carrier. Ships of the
Mediterranean were very different; they were constructed using plank-on-frame
techniques, with the hull planking butted edge-to-edge, that were cheaper, lighter
and required less skill of the builders. This technique is called 'skeleton' or 'carvel'
construction, and by the end of the thirteenth century much larger ships were being
built in the Mediterranean than anything seen in northern Europe. Records from
Genoa in 1268 tell us that three ships were built, each with three decks and a length
of more than 120 feet (36 metres), a 30-foot (9-metre) beam and a draught of 13 feet
(4 metres). These floating monsters were steered with two great side rudders, often
with pulley tackles to help the helmsman control his floating beast.

As trade increased between northern Europe and the Mediterranean ideas about shipbuilding evolved and developed. European and Mediterranean ships each had their strengths and weaknesses, and the carrack evolved from the best of both. By the middle of the fourteenth century the form of the carrack was well defined: it became a large, strongly built vessel, usually threemasted (but sometimes with as many as five), carrying two courses of square sails on the foremast and mainmast and a lateen sail – a triangular sail attached to a yard – on the short mizzenmast (the mast closest to the stern).

This evolution in ship design came about through a quite logical progression. Ships became bigger so that they could carry more cargo more economically. The carrack was carvel-built like the Mediterranean ships rather than clinker-built in the European style because it was cheaper, lighter and easier to build to such a design. The ships had a stern rudder like the cog rather than a side rudder as this gave better control, was easier to use and was less likely to be damaged in harbour. The lateen rig of the southern vessels gave way to the square rig from Europe. Although the square rig lacked the flexibility for coastal work, it required fewer crew members to handle and therefore left more room for cargo and was more suited to longer voyages. Several masts split the sails into more manageable sizes, which also allowed more sail area to be carried and made the vessel less vulnerable to demasting. The saving in crew wages was probably an important factor in the growing popularity of these ships. Venetian records of the thirteenth century state that each sailing ship should have one sailor for every ten *millaria* of cargo (about 5 tonnes); by the fifteenth century the requirement was one sailor for every twenty *millaria,* suggesting that a square-rigged ship needed only half the crew of a lateen-rigged ship of similar size.

Although the carrack developed into a large cargo-carrying vessel, often well over 100 feet (30 metres) in length, it was not particularly fast or weatherly. By the middle of the fifteenth century a smaller vessel evolved that had a range of uses: as a cargo carrier, a small warship or as a patrol or dispatch boat. This fast, weatherly, lightweight vessel was the caravel, and it became closely linked with the Portuguese and

THE HANSEATIC LEAGUE

The Hanseatic League was a federation of cities in northern Germany and communities of German merchants in the Low Countries, England and the Baltic. These merchant-cities organized themselves during the thirteenth century for protection and to promote their commercial interests.

At its peak the league was a powerful force in European politics. The federation developed in response to conditions that were unique to medieval Europe: the emergence of free cities and merchant guilds, the disintegration of centralized authority in Germany and the expansion of German trade and influence throughout Europe – not to mention the likelihood of meeting pirates along the main maritime trade routes.

An English manuscript from 1271 showing two hulks engaged in combat.
Naval strategy was crude during the middle ages and based on land battles. When within
range, archers would exchange arrows and missiles with the enemy. Once alongside, fore-
and aftcastles gave soldiers the advantage of height for close combat.

Spanish trans-oceanic explorations that led to the opening of a sea route to the East
Indies and the conquest of the New World.

Initially, these small, seaworthy ships carried lateen sails, similar to those of the
Arab dhow. This rig was ideal for coastal sailing, but as the great Portuguese and
Spanish explorations got under way they were converted to a square rig to make
them more suitable for trade-wind sailing, where a ship would normally run with the

63

wind directly behind her. The square rig also needed a smaller crew, which became a major consideration as expeditionary ships were often loaded with provisions for up to a year. The caravel was a relatively fine-lined craft that cut efficiently through the Atlantic swell. Its shallow draft was also a big advantage for surveying close inshore once new land had been discovered. The caravel is the best-known ship of the period, and Columbus took two on his first crossing to the West Indies in 1492; the smaller – the *Niña* – was his favourite. Unfortunately, no wreck of a fifteenth-century caravel has yet been found.

☉☉☉☉☉☉☉☉

This, then, was the boat that Colin Mudie had to design. With no plans, no pictures and very few historical references for the original *Matthew*, Mudie became involved in some historical detective work. He knew the size of the original, the tonnage and how many crew she carried. Historical research into ship design, combined with contemporary paintings and diaries, told him a lot about what the *Matthew* would have looked like and how she would have sailed.

Mudie's first assumption was that the ship was built or bought by an experienced mariner who intended to sail west across the cold and stormy waters of the North Atlantic Ocean into uncharted regions. The original would also have needed to be self-contained for as long as a year, so Mudie's next assumption was that she was a strong, weatherly, sea-going vessel and reasonably easy for the crew themselves to maintain. The *Matthew* sailed from Bristol down the notorious Bristol Channel, where the tides run very strongly – especially in the upper reaches and off headlands. The original vessel would therefore have been as good at sailing to windward (towards the prevailing wind) as any ship of the period. She would also have been able to dry out without risk of damage in case she ran aground and hence may have had a reasonably shallow draft. Ships using Bristol harbour were subjected to constant stresses and strains as they dried out at every low water, so the original *Matthew* could be expected to be well built from good-quality materials. Away from harbour ships relied on their sailing ability, but sailing ships are at their most vulnerable in light and failing winds while sailing close to shore. So, to navigate safely up and down the Bristol Channel the *Matthew* would have carried the largest sail area that was practical.

The tonnage of the *Matthew* is known from historical records. Although Cabot was sailing a shorter, more northerly route than Columbus, he would still have provisioned his ship to carry crew and equipment for up to a year, together with all the tools and materials needed to make repairs. To calculate the volume of the hull Mudie worked out what would have been required to carry supplies for the crew for a long period at sea. Fifteenth-century sailors did not have the benefit of tinned and frozen food and their diet was basic but bulky. There was also a veritable menagerie of livestock on board (at least in the early weeks) to provide fresh milk, eggs and meat. Mudie worked on the assumption that the ship carried food for at least six months but water for only three as this could obviously be replenished much more easily than food. Including spoilage in his calculations, he estimated that the food stores would have needed at least twice the volume that you would expect on a modern sailing ship.

A ship at sea for a year would need to have the rigging and sails replaced at least twice as the ropes and canvas of a medieval ship suffered badly from rot and stretch. On top of that room had to be found to stow a couple of lengths of replacement anchor rope, timber to replace (say) ten per cent of the planking plus some framing and warm clothing for a crew of nineteen men. Together, this adds up to a substantial amount of equipment to carry. The demands of a shallow, weatherly hull shape capable of meeting these requirements during the long passage across the north Atlantic and back led Mudie to design a hull with an overall length of just over sixty feet and a beam of twenty feet (18 metres long by 6 metres wide).

THE TON

The word 'ton' comes from the Old English word *tunne,* meaning a cask of liquid. In English medieval commercial and legal use this usually meant a wine barrel of 252 gallons (1147 litres) weighing approximately 2500 lb (1134 kilograms or about 1.1 modern tonnes).

Shipping 'tuns' are first mentioned in the thirteenth century and relate to the carrying capacity of a ship – the most important measure of its earning potential. In the fourteenth century the English crown used a ratio of approximately one man per four tons of ship to estimate the number of men required to crew vessels of more than 100 tons in royal service. Henry V built a monster royal ship in 1418 called the *Grace Dieu,* which weighed in at 1400 tons (and still lies at the bottom of the River Hamble near Southampton), but it is clear from port records that small ships predominated during this time and probably three-quarters of them displaced less than 100 tons.

☙☙☙☙☙☙☙☙☙

The shape of the hull was the next consideration. It was Henry VII's flagship the *Mary Rose* – which had been raised in 1982 and moved to a permanent site in Portsmouth dockyard – that gave the best clues to the underwater shape of the *Matthew.* The *Mary Rose* was built about ten years after the *Matthew* and had a hull shape that was more sophisticated than anything Mudie had previously imagined

Overleaf Although details have changed during construction, Colin Mudie's design study for the *Matthew* shows the basic accommodation. Forward, below decks, is the bosun's store. Aft, behind a watertight bulkhead, is the main accommodation with sixteen pipe cots for the crew, as well as the main engine. Aft, behind a second watertight bulkhead, is the galley port and starboard (the washroom or 'heads' was moved into the main cabin) and two more bunks. At deck level, in the aftcastle, is the Master's cabin and the navigation room, which also houses a mini-edit suite for the TV progammes.

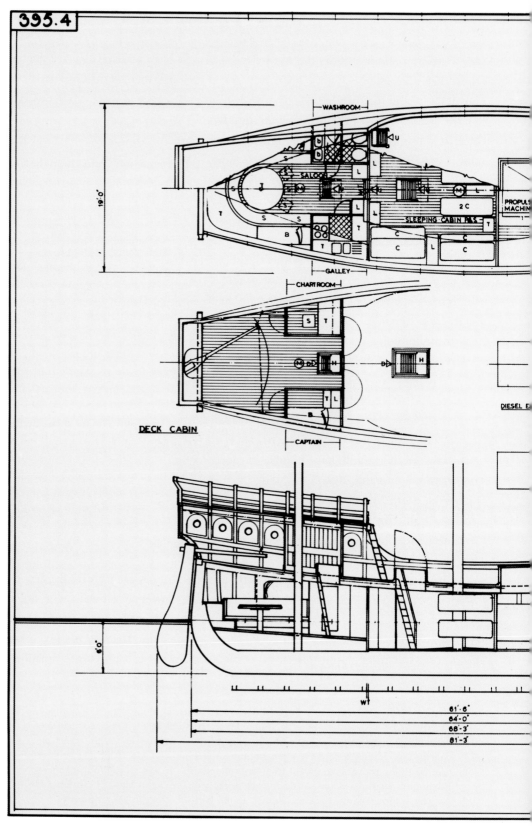

395.4

WASHROOM

19'-0"

SALOON

SLEEPING CABIN PASS

2 C

PROPULS
MACHIN

GALLEY

CHARTROOM

S   T

DECK CABIN

DIESEL E

CAPTAIN

6'-0"

Wt

61'-6"
64'-0"
68'-3"
81'-3"

MATTHEW

1997

DIMENSIONS

LOA (incl. bowsprit)	81 feet 3 inches
LOA	68 feet 3 inches
LOA (Hull)	64 feet
LWL (approx.)	61 feet 6 inches
KEEL	50 feet
BEAM	19 feet
DRAFT (approx.)	6 feet
DEPTH (approx.)	6 feet 6 inches
SAIL AREA	2360 square feet
DISPLACEMENT (approx.)	80 tons

UPPER DECK

LOWER DECK

KEY

b	BASIN
B	BERTH
C	COT
H	HATCH
L	LOCKER
M	MAST
S	SEAT
T	TABLE
WT	WT DOOR
◁U	UP
◁D	DOWN

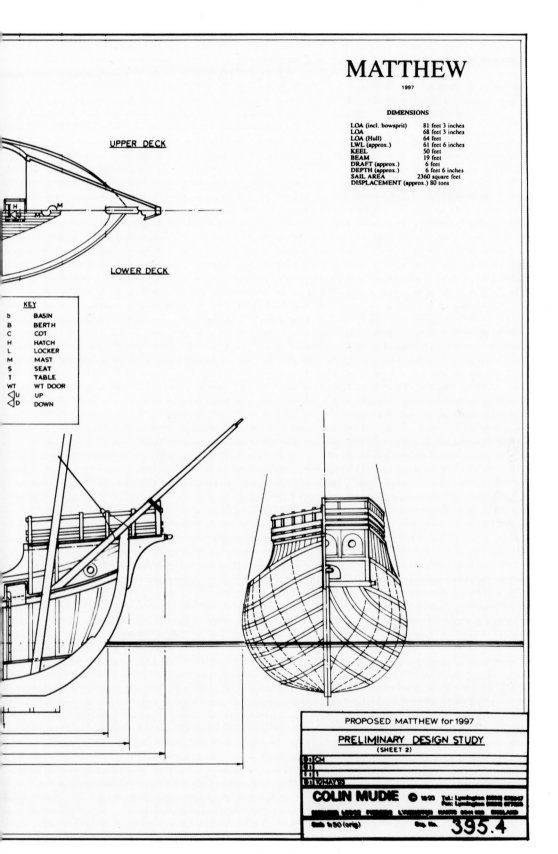

PROPOSED MATTHEW for 1997

PRELIMINARY DESIGN STUDY
(SHEET 2)

COLIN MUDIE © 10-93

Dg. No. 395.4

possible for the period. When the distorted flagship was 'realigned' to reveal the form of the original, he realized that the shape of her hull was very close to what scientists have developed to optimize 'laminar flow' and create 'lift'. To a ship designer this means, first, ensuring that the movement of water past the hull is as smooth and undisturbed as possible and, second, designing the hull to create 'lift', rather like an aircraft's wing. This was important in helping the boat to sail closer to the wind and to reduce leeway (the downwind 'slippage' through the water when a boat tries to sail into the wind; with ships like the caravel the leeway would have been 15 to 20 degrees, and even more in heavy weather).

THE MATTHEW - *The Known Facts*

The facts on which Colin Mudie based his design of the new *Matthew* were skimpy. From historical documents it was known that the ship had a displacement of around 50 tons, that she sailed from Bristol to Newfoundland in 34 days and returned in just 15 days, a remarkably fast easterly passage that must have been completed at an average speed of 5 knots. It was known that Cabot took a crew of eighteen or nineteen men and that the vessel was not only expected to cross oceans but would also have been used for exploration when it arrived.

Mudie claims that the hull of the *Mary Rose* is one of the most beautiful he has ever seen and that it had a considerable influence on his design of the underwater sections of the *Matthew*. Here was a boat with an efficient, bluff bow and a long, tapering fore-section that brought the maximum beam (width) aft of the middle of the boat, giving excellent load-carrying properties. This was a hull which could be sailed efficiently in all conditions, including the lightest of winds and without the benefit of an auxiliary engine. Mudie is convinced that the builders of these early sailing ships were highly skilled craftsmen who pushed their ideas and technologies to their limits. Their careers as shipwrights, the well-being of their families and even the success of nations depended on well-built ships. Mudie likens these people to the NASA space technicians of the age, building self-contained space capsules of the early Renaissance for voyages across the ocean into the unknown world beyond.

The most controversial part of the design of the *Matthew* was the shape of the stern. As with all ships, regardless of when they were built, the overall shape of a boat is limited by the materials and technology available to the builders. Until the time of construction of the original ship (and for a short time afterwards), one of the biggest limitations on the builder was the lack of good-quality, reliable fastenings that would stop timbers from being pulled apart. Today, boatbuilders use bolts and screws made from metals which will not rust at sea. Fifteenth-century boatbuilders had only crude iron nails, usually made on site by hammering raw iron. This process gave the nails a longitudinal porosity and they rusted easily, with disastrous consequences for those on board who were relying on a boat that held together! Fastenings that were placed under a shear stress rather than tension – in other words, those preventing timbers from pulling apart sideways – were easier to manufacture and could be made from timber; these were called 'treenails'. With a bit of cunning, boatbuilders of the period were able to make different styles of wooden fastening that could take light tension. But in general the builders of the *Matthew* were limited by having no adequate fastenings to stop pieces of wood from pulling apart.

This limitation contributed to major problems in building the stern. Most modern ships have a square stern, which gives extra beam to the hull and improves the carrying capacity; it also gives extra buoyancy and is relatively easy to build – provided that you can join the corners of the hull together. This option was not open to the builders of the *Matthew* and Mudie believes that the original was built with a rounded or pointed stern. This was how ships had been built since the Norman invasion, and the Viking longships and Greek galleys before them. By building a 'double-ender' the planking could be made to 'lock' into the stern post in a rebate (slot) and the construction did not have to rely on poor-quality iron fastenings. However, the decision to build a pointed stern was to cause difficulties for the builders and became a hot topic of conversation throughout the building.

The last major decision to be made on the design of the new *Matthew* was the rig – Mudie had to choose between a lateen and a square rig. When the caravel was first developed the sails were modelled on the Arab dhow and early versions carried lateen sails. This style sailed well to windward and was good for coastal navigation, but the lateen rig has several disadvantages for ocean sailing. It requires a bigger crew than the square rig, and a large crew means more space for provisions and hence more weight. The lateen rig is also under-canvassed, and Mudie was convinced that the *Matthew* would have carried plenty of sail for good light-weather performance. The lateen rig also tends to be unstable in a following wind. When Christopher Columbus first sailed the Atlantic in 1492, one of his two caravels, the *Niña,* carried a lateen rig. But he was so disappointed with her performance that when the expedition arrived in the Canary Islands he had the masts and spars cut down and rearranged as a square rig. This proved to be a much better configuration for sailing in the trade winds with the breeze behind the boat.

So Mudie designed the *Matthew* with a square rig, which he believes is both efficient and powerful. However, Cabot's outward voyage across the North Atlantic was *against* the prevailing winds. This decision by Mudie means that the crew of the new *Matthew* must learn sailing techniques that have lain dormant for a hundred years or more and will give the skipper, David Allan-Williams, and his twentieth century crew new challenges in sail handling and sailing technique.

⊚⊚⊚⊚⊚⊚⊚

CHAPTER 4

NEW FOR OLD

There was an Old Man in a boat,
Who said, 'I'm afloat! I'm afloat!'
When they said, 'No, you ain't!' he was ready to faint,
That unhappy Old Man in a boat.

EDWARD LEAR *The Book of Nonsense*

At the height of the Columbus celebrations in 1992 a local property surveyor and auctioneer (and Bristol Merchant Venturer) called St John Hartnell was asked by Bristol City Council to help celebrate Cabot's quincentenary by building a replica of the *Matthew*. People might be forgiven for thinking that trying to raise nearly £1.5 million in the middle of a major economic recession to build a wooden ship that few people had ever heard of was tantamount to madness. But Hartnell was determined and, like Cabot before him, he needed a sponsor. No support was forthcoming from local Bristol companies, so he used his contacts in the property development business and all his powers of persuasion to bring a backer on board. In the end it was an old friend, Mike Slade – a passionate yachtsman and head of a large property development company – who generously agreed to underwrite the project. This financial support was crucial because it allowed the building to proceed without problems of cash flow, which have caused similar projects to falter and fail in the past.

The go-ahead for Colin Mudie to work on the full design was finally given in November 1993. By February 1994 his line plans were ready and ten shipwrights, led by project manager Mike Blackwell, were able to start their work. Blackwell, a qualified surveyor who has run shipyards, has vast experience of the marine industry. The shipwrights were local men and experienced builders of wooden boats. Nevertheless, the experience of building a medieval replica was a novel one for them all.

Construction of the *Matthew* began in February 1994 on Redcliffe Quay. By the end of the year the overall shape could be seen: the hull is planked in Douglas fir on massive English oak frames. The caravel was carvel-built, which meant that the narrow gaps between the planks would have to be laboriously caulked before the launch.

Originally, mature oak trees which fell on the Longleat estate during the 1987 hurricane were earmarked for the ship. But fate intervened and the Longleat oaks were used to rebuild St George's Hall in Windsor Castle following the disastrous fire. Instead, oaks were selected from forests in Herefordshire and Gloucestershire. The new *Matthew* was built in the heart of Bristol at Redcliffe Quay, no more than a few hundred yards from the likely site where the original was built and directly in the early morning shadow of the magnificent medieval church of St Mary's, Redcliffe. A large semi-permanent canopy kept the site dry and created a visitors' centre that gave thousands of schoolchildren a glimpse of the mysterious world of the fifteenth century.

In May 1994 the keel was laid by HRH Prince Philip, who is patron of the project. The keel is the very backbone of a ship and by tradition, for a wooden vessel like the *Matthew,* it is cut from a single piece of mature oak. But today's trees do not have the stature of their fifteenth-century ancestors, so African opepe was used as a modern substitute. Fifty feet (15 metres) long and nearly two feet (0.5 metres) square, the massive keel weighed 1.5 tonnes and was laid across wooden blocks on the quay to allow the shipwrights access beneath to drive up the hull fastenings from below.

Meanwhile, a local warehouse was rented for space to fabricate the frames; here they were drawn full size on the warehouse floor – or 'lofted' – before each was accurately made to Mudie's plans. Trucked back to Redcliffe Quay, the frames were then erected on the wooden keel to create the overall shape of the vessel. At night, silhouetted against powerful lights, the oak frames of the *Matthew* stood out like the ribs of a giant beached whale. Next an inner keel, or 'keelson', was fitted above the main keel and bolted through, securing the bottom sections of the frames in a massive timber sandwich. The frames were cross-braced with beams, on which the decking would later be laid, and the beams were fixed in position with massive oak brackets called 'knees', each carefully fitted by hand. The strength of a wooden ship depends not only on the size of the timbers but also on the perfect fit of each individual piece, which is glued and through-bolted to 'lock' the framework into a massively strong structure. The final job before planking the hull and decks was fitting the 'wales'. These long, four-inch (100-mm) square oak timbers run the length of the outside of the hull; again, their purpose is to lock the frame of the ship into a single, sturdy structure.

Until this point construction had gone reasonably smoothly, but fitting the wales presented a serious problem to the builders. Mudie had designed a stern that was rounded, rather like a very bluff bow. This shape required the massive timbers to be bent around in a tight curve – a much tighter curve than the wood could normally be expected to accommodate. The traditional technique for curving timbers is literally to 'cook' them in a makeshift steam oven. The fire under the water container is lit, the planks are slid into the steaming box and the whole system bubbles away for hours at a time. As the timbers warm up in the hot, moist atmosphere they become flexible and can be bent easily. Once out of the steamer, the shipwrights had only a few minutes to get the 'steamed wale' into position and clamped before the timber cooled and went stiff again. Judging by the expletives which could be heard above the sound of hammering, the process was intensely frustrating for the builders, who snapped several pieces before they succeeded in getting the timbers fitted to their satisfaction. Even with the wales in position, 2.5-inch (63-mm) thick pine planking still had to be coaxed around the problematic stern, a task that proved to be one of the biggest challenges in building the *Matthew*.

The final shape of the vessel was sometimes changed during the building and the shipwrights often made small changes during construction, which resulted in a more authentic copy. This is how it would have been with the original vessel, for the *Matthew* was one of the last ships to be built before naval architecture became a recognized profession under the Elizabethans. Many skills and building techniques used on the original have since been lost, which partly explains the problems that were faced in building the replica. For example, Colin Mudie thinks that the builders might have used a traditional fire-burning technique to heat the stern planking to make it pliable enough to fit around the tight curves.

⊚⊚⊚⊚⊚⊚⊚

The original ship was built from English oak – the preferred timber of medieval boatbuilders. Good-quality oak was readily available in medieval England and could usually be found close to the building site, which reduced transportation costs. Oak is an excellent boatbuilding timber, described by John Evelyn, the seventeenth-century English diarist as: *'tough, bending all, strong and not too heavy, nor easily admitting water'*.[1] Tall forest oak with a long, straight grain and without low branches was used for the keel and long runs of planking. Trees of suitable shape produced naturally curved timbers for the frames, knees and other parts of the boat for which crooked sections were needed. Oak was used in huge quantities and the cutting and working of wood in the middle ages was a very labour-intensive exercise, so it was important for the master builder to select individual trees which best suited the job in hand and minimized the work involved in shaping. Sometimes forests were 'farmed' and individual trees were deliberately trained to specific shapes for shipbuilding.

The timbers for the *Matthew* probably came from the great oak forests of Wye and Dean on the English-Welsh border (see map on page 32) and would have been cut down in autumn and winter when the sap was no longer rising. Winter was the best time for felling as the trees had lost their leaves and their shapes could be seen easily; also, the undergrowth had died down and it was easier to move logs over hard-frozen ground. Another advantage was that, with the harvest over, more labourers were available. Although the working day was short, cold weather minimized the conditions in which rot could start in the timbers. Medieval ships were usually built from 'green' (unseasoned) oak and the trees and branches were roughly trimmed to size before moving them to the building site. Manually cutting tough English oak is hard labour even with modern hand tools; what it must have been like for medieval shipbuilders with their crude, iron saws, which could never hold an edge for long, almost defies imagination.

The timbers were moved from the forest by cart and boat. Although single pieces of a ton or more could be moved, timber was rarely transported more than ten or twenty miles (16–32 kilometres) over land. Contemporary reports suggest that a medieval ship required up to 500 cartloads of timber to build, and this was usually taken to the nearest navigable river for easier transportation to the construction site. If necessary, a track would be cut to the river and the wooden planks loaded on to a boat as close as possible to where the trees were being felled. The oak timbers for the *Matthew* would have been floated down the River Wye and into the Severn Estuary at Chepstow (see map on p32). From there, the river boatmen 'worked' the strong tides in the area: a single ebb tide would take the boats down the estuary to King Road, from where the following flood carried them up the River Avon and into the port of Bristol – a distance of fifteen or sixteen miles in a matter of hours. Some timbers might also have been supplied from smaller forests to the south of the city, but where possible they would all have been brought into Bristol by water. Sometimes the oak was temporarily stored under water to keep it fresh and moist, making it easier to work.

The building site for the original *Matthew* would have had little sophisticated equipment and the choice of site tended to be arbitrary. Bristol shipwrights were able to take advantage of the big tidal range in the city as it allowed them to excavate a 'dry dock' that could be flooded when construction of the ship was finished. The tidal dry dock was dug out alongside the harbour and closed with wooden gates, which were sealed with clay at low water. This ingenious system allowed the builders access to the hull at all times during construction. When the ship was completed the gates were opened and the new vessel could be floated out on the tide with no need for heavy lifting. Unfortunately, some shipbuilders did not bother to fill in their docks after use, creating a local hazard. The random digging of docks in Bristol in the mid-1470s eventually led to a local bye-law forbidding anyone without a permit 'to break any ground in and about Bristol to make any ship'.[2]

A close detail from *The Martyrdom of St Catherine*, Antwerp School *c*.1540.
This painting, possibly by Matthys Cock, shows shipbuilding and repair on a beach.
The two large carvel-built vessels on their sides are being 'careened' for caulking.
This involves drying out at low water to give access to the underwater sections of the
hull. The ship in the middle-right is being hauled over to one side using a beach-wind-
lass. In the background, the other ship is being caulked from a floating raft. Middle-left,
a third ship is under construction, surrounded by scaffolding to give the shipwrights
access as the hull is built up. (The stern of this ship is rounded, almost identical to the
new *Matthew*). To the left, sawyers are using trestles to cut timber; behind them,
a man appears to be boiling pitch over an open fire, probably for caulking. In the
centre-foreground another shipwright is using an adze to shape and smooth
a timber. The two small boats in the foreground appear to be clinker-built.

Building a wooden ship is always labour-intensive. Even with modern power tools and heavy lifting equipment the new *Matthew* took more than a dozen skilled shipwrights two years to complete. The medieval craftsmen had a more difficult task as they relied exclusively on hand tools. One of the most common medieval tools was the adze, which was used to shape and trim timbers. In experienced hands the adze is versatile and effective, and they were still used by the builders of the new *Matthew*. Chisels, hammers, pincers, long double-handed saws and augers for boring holes in timbers made up the rest of a medieval tool chest. Tools blunted quickly on the tough oak timbers and sometimes as many as ten replacement augers would be used during the building of a single ship.

Shipbuilding was not a particularly well-paid job and the medieval boatbuilder was part of a very distinct and rigid craft structure. They all served traditional apprenticeships, with pay that reflected their various skills. The least skilled was the servant, who might earn 1d a day; then, on 4d a day, came the holders, who literally held the nailheads on the outside of the hull. The clenchers (5d/day) crawled around inside the hull clenching over the points of the nails that came through the wood in clinker-built boats, and the shipwright berders (6d/day) fitted and shaped the timbers. At the top of the scale was the master shipwright, who would earn about 8d a day. Despite the low cost of labour, about 60 per cent of the cost of building a medieval ship was attributable to labour; interestingly, the proportion was much the same in the building of the new *Matthew*.

⊚⊚⊚⊚⊚⊚⊚

The final job before launching is to make the hull watertight – a constant preoccupation with all boatbuilders. The basic techniques that are used to 'caulk' a hull have not changed in five hundred years. The hull of the *Matthew* is carvel construction, where the planking is laid edge to edge and a small gap of approximately 0.25 inch (6 mm) is left between each plank. Before the vessel can be launched these gaps have to be filled or caulked, which is a laborious process. First, caulking cotton or oakum is gently hammered into the seam using a broad, chisel-shaped tool called a caulking iron. Caulking cotton is light, fluffy cotton string that is rolled into varying thicknesses; oakum is a heavier-duty tarred hemp but is used in much the same way. With the cotton or hemp tapped home, a stopping compound is trowelled over the seams and smoothed flush with the rest of the hull. When a wooden boat is launched it usually leaks at first, but once the caulking gets wet it swells, sealing the hull against further leaks. When the original *Matthew* was built, cotton had not been introduced to Europe from America and caulkers used other materials – oakum, wool, canvas or even moss – often mixed with tar before being rammed into the gaps between the planks.

Above Noah's Ark, from the *Nuremberg Chronicles*, 1493. This romanticized woodcut of the building of the Ark shows many of the common tools and techniques that would have been used on the construction of the original *Matthew*.

Overleaf left Construction of the *Matthew*. The futtocks were 8 inch square (20 cms) cut sections of English oak, bolted together to make the frames, or 'ribs' of the ship. The fastenings were aluminium bronze bolts.
Right: above The stempost weighed 2 tonnes and was supported with a timber tripod during construction. *Right: below* Inside, looking aft, clearly showing the tight curves made by the planking around the stern.

Colin Mudie's research into boats of the period suggested that the hulls were finished to a fine standard, varnished and decorated with brightly coloured panels along the topsides. Pictures from the fifteenth century often show a darker colour below the waterline, suggesting that the underside of the hull was given a protective coat of pitch or tar. This helped make the hull watertight and limited the growth of barnacles. Today the bottoms of ships are painted with anti-fouling preparations containing a poison that leaches out slowly, and these are much more effective at preventing the growth of marine animals on the hull.

By September 1995 the replica of the *Matthew* was ready for the water.

❦❦❦❦❦❦❦

The builders of the original *Matthew* had a much easier time launching their ship – they simply broke the mud seals and opened the gates of the tidal dock and waited for the water to flood in at high tide. The launch of the new *Matthew* was altogether a more elaborate affair. The morning of the launching day on 9 September 1995 dawned bright and clear, much to the relief of the organizers. A stiff westerly wind picked up the flags and coloured bunting, making the event a spectacular occasion. It was an important day for the people of Bristol, who had watched 'their' ship grow from a pile of timber to something that was recognizable as a medieval vessel. Twenty thousand people watched from the quays as the great and the good of Bristol assembled for the ceremony. The Band of the Royal Marines struck up their marching music as Lady Wills, wife of the Lord Lieutenant of Avon, cut the ribbon and officially launched the *Matthew* with a traditional blue bottle of Bristol Sherry – the choice of wine was made at the last minute and proved a very popular decision with the people of Bristol.

The day belonged to Mike Blackwell and the shipwrights. Blackwell supervised the launch in a set of new white overalls. Once the bottle was broken over the bows, he gave the signal and 40 tons of African opepe, English oak and Douglas fir was lifted high above Redcliffe Quay and lowered gently into the murky waters of Bristol harbour. Amid all the applause, the brass band and the deafening explosions of the live gun salute, a nervous figure in white clambered on board and hastily checked the bilge; five minutes later a relieved Mike Blackwell reappeared to announce that the hull was tight and making only a small amount of water – exactly what he had expected. That night Bristol rang to the sound of music and party-making as the organizers celebrated with a formal ball for their guests.

The launch was more of a public relations exercise than anything. It marked an important stage in the construction for the people of Bristol, but it also raised the profile of the project in the local and national papers and on television – and it was a chance for the organizers to try to entice a few more sponsors on board.

As the following Monday morning dawned and the hangovers subsided, the *Matthew* was unceremoniously lifted back on to Redcliffe Quay and the long process of fitting out began. The sails were ordered and the rigging made. The main mast was hewn from a solid pine trunk more than four feet (1.2 metres) in diameter (it took one shipwright three months simply to turn the mast from a square to a round section). The castles were built and decked over and two small cabins were constructed aft – a small chartroom and the skipper's cabin. The interior was fitted out with sixteen bunks for the crew and a galley was built with a large oven and refrigerator; a huge bank of batteries powered the very latest in electronic navigation equipment and was charged by a 240-hp diesel engine.

The choice of drive units caused great consternation on the building site. Early one morning in February 1996 two big wooden crates were delivered, each containing an outdrive pod with a large bronze propeller. These were to be driven by a massive hydraulic pump attached to the engine. The advantage of such a system is that it allows the propellers to be located independently of the main engine, connected by heavy-duty piping through which hydraulic fluid is pumped under high pressure. However, on inspection these ungainly looking pods looked wrong for the job, so the suppliers were called and told they had delivered the incorrect units. It turned out that the order was right but that a decision had been made at a late stage to fit a different type of propeller unit more suited to steel-hulled vessels. The builders were not happy about fitting the drive pods, which required last-minute alterations to reinforce the stern sections.

The units proved to be a hazard on a voyage from Bristol to Ireland in June 1996, when the pipes leaked hydraulic fluid into the bilges and the *Matthew* had to be towed ignominiously into harbour by the Ballycotton lifeboat. The units also made themselves universally unpopular with the crew as they were so noisy that anyone working in the aft cabin for more than a few minutes when the ship was under power had to wear industrial ear-defenders.

@@@@@@@@

Overleaf The *Matthew* during sea trials in 1996, seen from halfway
up the rigging. On the left is the raised aftcastle where the helmsman and
watchkeeper have an unrestricted view forward. Top of picture are the 'ratlines'
or rope ladders attached to the mainstays, which give the strong-hearted access to the
crow's nest. To the right is the lower 'waist' or central section of the vessel.
During heavy weather, this area is awash as the ship rolls in big seas.

A cause of surprise to many visitors is that the *Matthew* has an engine at all. People's initial reaction is that the boat should remain true to the original and not have any mechanical power. However, the reality of financing and building a replica medieval ship is far removed from such glossy-eyed idealism. Organizing a project of this nature is serious business, employing at times dozens of people and with nearly £2 million invested. The new *Matthew* has to earn her keep – just like the original ship. But the twentieth century makes greater demands on time-keeping than the fifteenth century and there was not even time to complete the fitting-out before the *Matthew* left Bristol in March 1996 to sail to London for important sponsorship events. This was only the beginning of a gruelling schedule of maritime festivals throughout the summer of 1996, which included the International Festival of the Sea in Bristol, plus other sailing festivals in Ireland and France, before her final public appearance of the year at Cowes Week. The reality is that the ship could only maintain this schedule by travelling between venues under power, and between March and December 1996, the engine logged 800 hours.

Nor would the ship have been economically viable if she was built in the traditional manner, with unseasoned oak held together by wooden 'treenails'. Like the original *Matthew,* she would have had a life expectancy of ten, perhaps twenty years at most. Instead, the new vessel is held together by high-quality (and very expensive) bronze bolts and the latest in marine glue; with the proper maintenance she could still be around for the 600th anniversary. Cabot himself would have envied the quality of the twentieth-century *Matthew.*

He might also have appreciated – not to say marvelled at – the navigational aids carried on board. Modern lightweight radar, VHF and short-wave radios, a satellite navigation system that gives an instant fix anywhere in the world to within 100 metres and electronic chart plotters all add up to increased safety for the nineteen souls who will sail the Atlantic in the summer of 1997. The challenge is serious enough without taking unnecessary risks and safety considerations have always had the highest priority on the new *Matthew.* The sails are polyester and the ropes of man-made fibre, a vast improvement on the hemp of Cabot's day, when the rigging would have been replaced every few months – if it did not rot and fall apart sooner.

The other big advantage the new vessel has over the old is the ballast. Cabot's ship would have had rock and gravel in the hold to give it the stability to withstand sideways forces from the wind on the sails. The bulky rock would have left barely five feet of headroom in the foul-smelling hold and it could move during a knock-down or capsize at sea – with disastrous consequences. On the grounds of stability alone his ship would never have met modern safety standards. The new *Matthew* had 29 tonnes of lead ingots strapped into the bilges after she was launched, and even this improvement over Cabot's day produced a vessel whose stability was barely adequate by today's requirements. There is little doubt that a truly authentic replica of the *Matthew* would have been a potentially unstable and dangerous ship by modern standards – and one which would in any case have fallen apart after little more than a decade.

◎◎◎◎◎◎◎

1996 was always intended to be a year of testing and sea trials for the *Matthew*. Apart from the trouble with the hydraulic drive units, other problems became apparent during the summer. So, after her last public appearance at Cowes Week, the ship went into a yard on the Hamble for a comprehensive refit. The unpopular drive units were replaced by more conventional hydraulic gearboxes. The rudder was altered to improve her handling characteristics and her masts were removed and lightened to improve stability. The rigging was overhauled and all working systems were checked and double-checked. The boat had originally been varnished; although she looked elegant, varnish is not a tough coating and ropes rubbing on the ship's timbers had produced ugly marks. So the exterior was laboriously sanded down to bare wood and a couple of dozen coats of a special Norwegian oil treatment were painstakingly applied by volunteers working at the weekend. The oil had the dramatic effect of bringing out the full, rich colours of the timbers, which now looked magnificent. The living accommodation was also stripped out and rebuilt to an improved design. Overall, the refit increased the safety of the ship and provided the crew with better living conditions.

One of the more controversial decisions taken during the refit was to fit an external keel to the hull. Ten tonnes of lead ballast was moved from inside the hull and refitted to the outside of the keel. This was intended to improve both the sailing qualities and the stability of the ship. However, with an external keel – which is a relatively recent innovation in ship design – the new *Matthew* will sail and handle in a very different way to the original ship. Many believe that the main reason for building such replicas is to create a piece of living history so that we can learn first-hand about how the original ships were sailed. Purists will argue that this opportunity has now been lost.

In all, it was a very expensive refit which put even greater stresses on the finance of the project and increased the need for additional sponsorship. But when the *Matthew* was relaunched in November 1996 and sailed back to spend the winter in Bristol the lessons of the summer had been learnt and the ship was ready at last to take on the full might of the North Atlantic.

◎◎◎◎◎◎◎

CHAPTER 5

ACROSS THE WESTERN SEA

They sailed to the Western Sea, they did, –
To a land all covered with trees:
And they bought an owl, and a useful cart,
And a pound of rice, and a cranberry-tart,
And a hive of silvery bees …

EDWARD LEAR *The Jumblies*

Christopher Columbus is usually given credit for being the first person to 'discover' America, but he never actually set foot on the American mainland. In fact, John Cabot has a stronger claim to be regarded as the founding father of the continent. Yet neither was the first European to land on American soil, North or South, for the remarkable history of trans-Atlantic exploration can be traced back a thousand years or more before Columbus and Cabot.

The first people to discover the American continent were nomadic hunters from Asia. They followed herds of mammoth, musk-ox and caribou across the Bering land bridge between Asia and North America 35,000 years ago, when the global sea level was lower during a cold climatic period. These hunter-people spread south and east throughout the Americas, diversifying into dozens of native American groups. The first to settle in Newfoundland were the Red Paint people around 2000BC. They lived there until around 1200BC, then suddenly disappeared. Newfoundland was settled again from the north by the Dorset Eskimos, who migrated from Greenland and Baffin Island, but they too disappeared from the island in around AD750.

The *Matthew* on her final voyage of 1996, when she sailed from Plymouth to Bristol in mid-December. She is carrying her full complement of sail, except for the bonnets on the mainsail and the foresail. The bonnets were not set in case of bad weather, when sail area would need to be reduced at short notice.

When John Cabot landed in Newfoundland in 1497 he found signs of Indians – the Beothuk – who survived on the island for nearly a thousand years before being officially declared extinct in 1829. The Beothuk were hunter–gatherers and numbered between 500 and 1000 in 1497. They were good canoeists who hunted seals with primitive harpoons and fished for salmon and shellfish; they were equally at home in the woods, tracking deer with bows and arrows. They used birch bark to make cooking vessels and wigwams and smeared red ochre on their skin, both for religious reasons and to protect themselves against insects. It is probably because of this custom that native Americans were called 'Red Indians' by the Europeans. Their pestering of white fishermen eventually led to the French putting a bounty on their heads. The last known Beothuk, Nancy Hawanahdit, died in 1829.

◎◎◎◎◎◎◎

In the sixth century, during the so-called 'Dark Ages', Christian monks lived in isolated communities and sought solitude in ambitious voyages around the coast of Europe. The monastery on the Inner Hebridean island of Iona developed from one such voyage by St Columba, who landed there in AD563. Irish monks in particular travelled very widely, and the most famous of them all was the legendary St Brendan (or Brandon) of Clonfert. Brendan was born around AD489 in Tralee in county Kerry; he was educated by local monks and in time became a monk himself, eventually founding a monastery in what is now Clonfert, in county Galway. Brendan liked to travel and he developed quite a reputation for long journeys to the western and northern islands of Scotland, the Færoe Islands and Brittany. He might also have travelled to continental Europe and to the Canary Islands – then known as the Fortunate Isles. In the sixth century these exploits alone would have been remarkable. But for Brendan it was just the beginning.

A monk called Barrind visited Clonfert and told Brendan of a distant country which he called the 'Promised Land of the Saints'. Brendan was determined to visit this far-off land and at the age of seventy he set sail with a group of fellow monks in a leather *curragh* to find this distant place. The voyage lasted seven years and St Brendan is thought to have sailed to Newfoundland via Iceland and Greenland. His travels are recorded in a popular medieval romance, *Navigatio Sancti Brendani Abbatis*, or *The Voyage of Saint Brendan*, which tells of his fabulous adventures. At least 120 manuscripts in the original Latin survive; none dates from the time of the original voyage, but they might have been written as early as AD800. This detailed chronicle tells amazing stories of a sea monster spouting foam from its nostrils, of a rocky and barren island where the travellers were pelted with slag and of a pillar of bright crystal that rose from the sea and was so large that it took three days just to sail up to it.

St Brendan and his monastic crew during their voyage to North America.
Brendan's voyage is told in the popular medieval romance, *Navigatio Sancti Brendani Abbatis,* which describes their amazing experiences, including a sea monster that spouted foam from its nostrils. In the top of the picture is the fictitious St Brendan's Isle, and to the bottom left the Fortunate Islands which Brendan is reputed to have visited during a previous voyage.

These stories might have remained no more than a medieval fairy tale were it not for the explorer-historian Tim Severin. In the true spirit of Thor Heyerdahl and other explorer-historians, he wanted to test the idea that St Brendan's story was based on true events. Severin approached Colin Mudie in the mid-1970s to design a reconstruction of Brendan's boat; the result was an extraordinary vessel made from 49 hand-sewn oxhides, each 4 feet by 3 feet (1.2 metres by 0.9 metres), tanned in oak bark and stretched over a lattice frame of Irish ash. The *Brendan* could be rowed and could also be sailed downwind using a flax mainsail set on a single mast.

Severin and his crew set off on St Brendan's day in 1976 and faced many difficulties and dangers on the voyage, including gales, persistent cold and dampness, swamping, and several encounters with whales – who seemed to develop quite an affinity with this strange, oxhide boat. But the greatest threat came quite late in the voyage from ice floes, which punctured the skin of their frail craft. They only avoided sinking by leaning over the side and laboriously sewing on patches by hand in the freezing waters of the North Atlantic. The crew finally arrived in Newfoundland in the summer of 1977. By coincidence, the first boat to sight the *Brendan* off the coast of Newfoundland was a Canadian coastguard ship called the *John Cabot*.

Many of the incidents recounted in the *Navigatio* have been reinterpreted in the light of Severin's voyage: the sea monster was probably the monks' first sighting of a whale; the land which pelted slag was an erupting volcanic island off Iceland; and the description of the huge crystal is possibly the first written account of an iceberg. St Brendan spoke of the 'Promised Land' as being 'fog-enshrouded',[1] something which is common off the coast of Newfoundland. Severin now believes that Irish monks were quite capable of crossing the Atlantic to North America in the sixth century. It may be that the *Navigatio* is not simply a story of a single voyage by St Brendan and his crew but a tale of several – perhaps many – voyages by Irish monks at that time.

Whether Brendan actually made his voyage is secondary to the fact that in the Middle Ages he was widely believed to have done so. The medieval romance of the *Navigatio* had a significant influence on early cartographers and, from the fifteenth century, mapmakers included the fabled St Brendan's Island on their Atlantic charts. Generations of mariners in the 1400s therefore grew up believing that land lay over the Western Ocean, where it only waited to be rediscovered.

☙☙☙☙☙☙☙

Around the turn of the first millennium, new trans-Atlantic explorers appeared on the scene who could not have been a greater contrast to the gentle Irish monks – the infamous Norsemen of Scandinavia. The Norse were pagans with a reputation for being quarrelsome and sexually promiscuous, but they were also skilled ocean sailors. Coastal transport was an important part of the Norwegian economy and by the eighth century the British Islands, France and the Low Countries were falling victim to Norse raiding parties. Not surprisingly, a new word entered the English language – *Viking*. The word means a man from the Vik (the arm of the North Sea fringed by southern Norway, western Sweden and Denmark now called the Skagerrak), but in practice it became a pejorative term meaning any Norseman on the hunt for plunder.

The Vikings were the scourge of northern Europe for more than two hundred years, penetrating inland in their dragon-bowed longships in search of settlements to rob. Favourites with the raiders were the monasteries of the Celtic Church, which contained riches beyond the dreams of ordinary Norsemen. Before long the monks of the British Islands were reciting a new prayer: *A furiori Normanorum, libera nos, Domine* (From the fury of the Northmen, deliver us, O Lord!). Their concern was well placed – one technique used by the Vikings was to slit open a man's chest and spread out his lungs like the wings of a bird: it was called a blood-eagle.

It was during this period of terror in Europe that the Norse began their voyages across the Atlantic. They were coastal navigators by nature but quite capable of making short passages out of sight of land. They used the Atlantic islands like giant stepping stones: the Orkneys, Shetland, Scotland, the Hebrides and Ireland; no leg was more than 600 miles (950 kilometres). The voyages were mainly undertaken in summer when the days were long and the winds benign. The Norse could also measure the angle of the sun, allowing them to sail fairly accurately in an east–west direction. By AD870 they had settled in Iceland among the Irish colonists who had preceded them two centuries earlier during the Brendan period of travels. The Norse drove the Irish from Iceland, and these Celtic refugees became the first Europeans to settle in Greenland.

The saga of Eirik Thorvaldsson is the first that tells of the colonization of North America. Eirik, son of Thorvald, had hair and a beard of such a flaming colour that by the age of fifteen he was given the nickname Eirik the Red. Eirik left Norway in AD963 with his father and the rest of his family, together with assorted breeding animals and other essential goods, and sailed for Iceland.

These voyages west were tough and the loss of life was high. Eirik's family sailed in a knarr, which had greater freeboard (a term referring to the height of the deck or hull above the waterline) and was more heavily built than the longboats used by the Vikings for raiding. They were open boats, sixty to eighty feet (18–24 metres) long and carrying twenty or thirty people together with their belongings and animals. They had a single mast and a square sail of wool, which makes poor sailcloth, but the Norse sewed strips of walrus-hide across the sail in a criss-cross pattern to stop it

THE NORSE SAGAS

These medieval Icelandic stories were written mainly in the late twelfth and thirteenth centuries and recount the exploits of Icelandic heroes who lived around AD900–1050. The literal meaning of the Old Norse word *saga* is 'what is said'. The main heroes were ordinary people such as farmers – people similar to the intended audience. Because the sagas were passed orally through several generations before being written down, versions of the same event tend to differ with different writers, and the style of the saga often reflects the style of a particular storyteller. Although some are largely fictional, other sagas contain valuable information on the exploration of the North Atlantic.

stretching. The knarr could not sail closer than at right-angles to the wind and an ocean voyage was dangerous and uncomfortable. Sometimes a small tent was erected in the middle of the boat for protection or people huddled together to escape the worst of the weather in tiny 'cuddies' (cabins) at each end of the vessel. They survived on dried or smoked meat and fish eaten cold, perhaps with some fruit or berries.

Once in Iceland there was cod in abundance. This was gutted, salted lightly and laid out to dry in the open, producing a desiccated, almost mummified slab of hard, dry, golden-coloured fish that kept well for up to a year. Otherwise, it was a hard life of subsistence farming and food was scarce. Timber was also in short supply, so the Norse lived in long houses built from turf or peat alternating with stones to give the structure strength.

Eirik married in Iceland and in due course a son, Leif, was born. It was not long before Eirik fell out with the neighbours; in true Norse style a lot of blood was shed on both sides before he was banished from the country. So, in AD982, Eirik set sail with his young family for a continent that lay just 175 miles (280 kilometres) to the west and which could be seen on a good day from Iceland's mountain tops. The voyage took them to a land Eirik called 'Grønland' (Greenland) because, as the sagas reported: *'he said that people would be much more tempted to go there if it had an attractive name'*.[2] There the family found summer pastures and salmon in the clear rivers that ran from the glaciers. Excavations of the Norse settlement in the 1920s revealed signs of still earlier buildings with floor plans very similar to those of Irish farmhouses of the Dark Ages, suggesting that the house had been built by Irish monks – possibly as a refuge after fleeing Iceland when the Norse arrived two generations earlier.

Greenland lacked the timber and iron essential for boatbuilding, but Eirik was undaunted and he established two Norse communities. The immigrants survived by breeding cattle, fishing and sealing; they exported furs, and narwhal ivory (which they claimed was unicorn horn, widely believed to have aphrodisiac properties), white falcons, which were greatly prized in medieval Europe, and walrus tusks – which became the most important export from this inhospitable land where life was even harder than in Iceland.

In AD985 a trader called Bjarni Herjolfsson sailed from Iceland with a loaded knarr intending to barter with the people of Greenland. On the third day, the favourable easterly wind increased in strength and backed to the north; he had little option but to run before the storm, presumably with the crew bailing as best they could from the open boat. In storm conditions a knarr will drift downwind at 5 knots or more, even with no sails set – equivalent to 120 miles (190 kilometres) a day or more. The sagas say the storm lasted 'many days', and when it was over Herjolfsson was well to the south of Greenland. Turning west, the crew eventually sighted land low on the horizon; it was thickly forested and looked very different from Iceland or Greenland.

Herjolfsson chose not to go ashore but turned north, sighting land a second and a third time. Navigating by the Pole Star, he continued north until confident that they were on the same latitude as southern Greenland, and then he turned due east. Four days later the knarr arrived in southern Greenland. Herjolfsson's first sighting was probably southeastern Newfoundland and his second and third the coast of Labrador. He was the first Norseman to discover North America, and his voyage was a fine example of seamanship and superb deductive navigation.

The Norse community in Greenland could not survive long without a supply of boatbuilding timber. Bjarni Herjolfsson's discoveries became part of the settlers' folk-lore and, in AD1001, a new voyage was organized by Leif Eiriksson, Eirik's son. The Greenlander's saga tells how Leif sailed with thirty-five men to an icy, barren land they called Helluland (literally 'Slab Land'); farther south they made landfall in a flat, wooded region which they named Markland ('Forest Land'); again they sailed south, and this time they reached another wooded area that was rich beyond their dreams. The hills were covered with fine boatbuilding timber, the rivers teemed with salmon, wild wheat grew in abundance and the flat land was rich pasture. Eiriksson called the place Vinland.

The exact locations of the three landfalls are not known, but Vinland was almost certainly in Newfoundland, Markland was Labrador, and Helluland, the glaciated Baffin island. The expedition settled in Vinland, built long houses and spent an easy first winter in North America before returning to Greenland loaded with timber.

In AD1003 Leif lent his brother Thorvald his knarr for another expedition. Thorvald took about thirty men back to the winter camp on Vinland, but the expedition was a disaster. Their ship was damaged and they were attacked by the local Indians, who they called *skraelings,* or 'wretches'. Thorvald fell to an unlucky arrow and died. Various expeditions returned for fish, fur and timber over the next two hundred years, but skirmishes with the Indians and with each other led to the Norse abandoning their settlement. After about AD1200 climatic changes brought on a mini ice-age which clogged the waterways and forced the seal herds and fish farther south. The Norse abandoned Greenland sometime around AD1300.

Overleaf A romanticized painting of Viking sea raiders by the late-Victorian artist, Albert Goodwin (1845-1932). The Vikings were the scourge of Europe for over two hundred years as they penetrated deep inland in their dragon-bowed longships. Bristol was attacked on more than one occasion by raiders who sailed far up the Severn Estuary. A major Viking centre in the west of the British islands was in Ireland at a place where the dark bog water made a 'black pool', called *Dyfflin* in Norse, or *Dubh Linn* in Irish.

CLIMATIC CHANGE

Climatic conditions during the Norse explorations were much warmer than today. Around AD1000–1250 a warm interval peaked in what is called the Early Medieval Warm Period. The favourable climate aided the wide-ranging voyages of the Norsemen: the polar ice-caps melted, raising global sea level and making it easier for the Norse boats to travel inland. For example, between the eighth and tenth centuries the Vikings travelled as far as the Crimea.

Later, voyages to North America were possible because the westerly storm tracks across the Atlantic shifted farther north, sea ice was less common and conditions were generally milder, making sailing in the North Atlantic easier than it is today. The warmer conditions allowed the Norse to establish their settlements in Iceland, southern Greenland (Eirik the Red, AD985) and in eastern North America (Vinland; Leif Eiriksson, AD1001).

Evidence for these warmer conditions comes from many sources. In Alaska, tree rings suggest that the mean temperature was 2–3°C warmer in the eleventh century than it is today, allowing Eskimos to settle in Ellesmere Island in the extreme north around AD900. An increase in rainfall in the semi-arid southwestern part of the North American continent led to increased vegetation growth and allowed supported agriculture; Pueblo campsites in the region can be dated at around AD1100–1200. The snow line in the Rocky Mountains was about 1000 feet (300 metres) higher than today, and similar trends are recorded in Australia and Chile. Still farther afield, records kept in Japan suggest that cherry was blossoming early in the twelfth century.

@@@@@@@@@@

In 1963 the remains of long houses and Norse artefacts were found at L'Anse-aux-Meadows in northeastern Newfoundland, and these have been dated at around AD1000 – the very time of the visits outlined in the sagas. Then, in 1965, the 'Vinland Map' was discovered, apparently dating from AD1440, showing both imaginary and real islands west of the European continent. These include Iceland, Greenland and the *'Island of Vinland, discovered by Bjarni and Leif in company'*.[3] The authenticity of the map has been disputed, but this does not detract from the certainty that the Norse settled briefly in North America at the turn of the millennium.

@@@@@@@@

By the fourteenth century, trade began to increase throughout Europe and the coastline from Gibraltar to Norway and Iceland began to be charted. Consequently knowledge of the Norsemen's attempts to settle in the western lands began to be shared throughout the royal courts of Norway, Denmark, Sweden and even England. We know, for example, that the king of Denmark (who also ruled Greenland and Iceland) appealed to the Pope in the thirteenth century to reduce the taxes levied on Greenland because of a poor harvest, so Rome knew at least of the existence of the country. The Danish king also complained about English pirates in Greenland waters in the fourteenth century. Basque whalers from northern Spain and southern France frequently fished as far north as Iceland and beyond. As early as 1372, fishermen were paying taxes to the Spanish crown on whales taken in waters off Labrador and Newfoundland.

Greenland is two hundred miles (320 kilometres) from the North American coastline, and, as Bjarni Herjolfsson found in AD985, this is only a couple of days running before a northeasterly gale. So it is quite possible that English pirates and Basque fishermen were not infrequent visitors to the coast of Newfoundland whether they chose to go there or not! Columbus spoke to Basque sailors in the Azores before he sailed in 1492, and Cabot too knew of the Basque fishermen. The Portuguese sailor Vaz Corte Real sailed to Greenland in 1476 and may have sighted the coastlines of Labrador and Newfoundland; he called the land he saw 'Terra do Bacalhao', or Land of Salt Cod. On returning the expedition gave a detailed account of the voyage that was widely circulated around the courts of Europe.

What is clear from all these little-reported voyages is that by the second half of the fifteenth century sailors from all the European maritime nations were accumulating knowledge and understanding of the northern and western parts of the Sea of Darkness. The time was close for serious exploration.

☺☺☺☺☺☺☺☺

Of all the tentative explorations across the Atlantic during the middle of the fifteenth century, the most determined were made by the fishermen and merchants of Bristol. In 1412 *'fishermen of England'* were reported off Dyrholm in Iceland;[4] exactly where they came from is not recorded, but by 1436 the venturesome mariners of Bristol were certainly sailing to the island:

> Of Iceland to write is little need, save of stock-fish:
> Yet forsooth indeed, out of Bristol, and coasts many a one,
> Men have practised by needle and by stone
> Thitherwards within a little while within twelve years,
> And without peril gone and come ...[5]

This *Libelle* published in 1436 suggests that Bristol and Iceland were trading at least as early as 1424, mainly for cod (the 'stock-fish' mentioned in the extract and described in

Overleaf A three-masted carrack anchored off the port of Antwerp during the zenith of the Hanseatic League. This panoramic view of the river Sheldt dates from 1468, and shows how busy major European ports were during the fifteenth century. A large treadmill-powered harbour crane can be seen lying alongside the quay, centre-left.

bargchinhoff

berßhott

Gatronßen

Nadmolen

horoßt

bedaindeß

the boxed article below). Bristol ships returned north packed with cloth, wool, beer, wine and everyday household items: it was a lucrative business for the Bristol merchants. But it was not long before this profitable trade came to the attention of the Hanseatic League – the Baltic cartel of merchants who controlled most of the trade in northwestern Europe. Anyone trading in Icelandic stockfish was obliged to pay dues and to trade only through the port of Bergen in Norway – which was hardly a practical proposition for the merchants of Bristol. Sometimes the Bristol merchants obtained special permits granting them dispensation, but more often they resorted to smuggling. Customs records (which can still be seen in the Public Record Office in London) contain valuable information on ships calling at British ports during this period, their cargoes and destinations, but they only give part of the story because of the inevitable 'unofficial' trade between Bristol and Iceland.

This remunerative trade between Bristol and Iceland was a thorn in the side of the Hanseatic League. In 1467 hostilities broke out between the League and England; the Hanse seized four English ships for illegal trading and the English retaliated by arresting all the Hanseatic merchants in London. The situation quickly developed into an all out trade war – the first Icelandic cod war in history. Within a few years a peace treaty was signed, but future trade with Iceland was vulnerable and the merchants of Bristol needed a more reliable source of cod.

When tensions with the Hanse were still running high, a Bristol ship sailed in 1480 on an exploratory voyage into the Atlantic. Our knowledge of this little-known expedition comes from the notebook of a Bristol merchant called William Worcestre:

> 1480. On the 15th day of July the ship belonging to [name missing] and
> John Jay junior, of 80 tons burthen, began a voyage from the port of Bristol
> at King Road to the Island of Brasil to the west of Ireland ...[6]

The gaps in Worcestre's jotting are frustrating, but the message is clear. Twelve years before Columbus sailed for the Indies, the merchants of Bristol may already have

---

STOCKFISH

Fifteenth-century Europe was staunchly Catholic – the excommunication of Martin Luther and the Reformation of the Church were still two generations away. So fish was an important part of people's diet and meatless days made up a third of the year. This created a constant demand, but fresh fish was a luxury and most people ate salted or dried fish. North Atlantic cod was easier and cheaper to preserve than other fish like the oily herring as it required only light salting before being laid out in the sun and wind to dry. Nor did dried cod need expensive barrelling, making it a cheaper alternative to local fish. Bristol merchants imported the cured product – known as 'stockfish' – from Iceland, where they sold cloth, beer, wine and everyday household items in return. It was a lucrative trade.

---

been looking west across the Atlantic for new trading opportunities. It is known that the voyage had backing from Edward IV, who issued a licence in June 1480 giving royal assent for two or three Bristol ships of 60 tons or under *'to trade for three years to any parts with any except staple goods'*.[7]

However, the voyage was not a success. Worcestre wrote in his diary:

> … and news came to Bristol on Monday 18 September that the said ship had … found no island and had been forced back by storms at sea …[8]

The merchants of Bristol were undeterred. The next year another voyage was undertaken, this time with two ships, the *Trinity* and the *George*. Both ships apparently returned safely, but there is no record of whether the voyage was a success or not. However, each ship reported loading a cargo of forty bushels of salt (nearly 1.5 tons) which is a lot for a ship to carry as salt was normally imported through Bristol, not exported. The ship's owner, Thomas Croft (a Bristol merchant), claimed that the salt was for the ship's *'repair, equipment and maintenance'* and that it was taken *'not with the intention of trading'* but for *'examining and finding a certain island called the Isle of Brasil'*.[9]

It is possible that Bristol merchants were fishing off the Grand Banks southeast of Newfoundland even before the 1480 voyage to 'Brasil' reported by William Worcestre and that the *George* and the *Trinity* were in fact carrying large quantities of salt to preserve cod caught on the Banks and to resupply a base on the North American mainland. If so, the Bristol merchants had every reason to keep the fledgling trade a secret. In 1480 the relationship between England and the Hanseatic League was still tense and the harbour in Bristol, like every other busy port in Europe, had ears. England's competitors – the League, Spain, Portugal, France and the Italian city-states, such as Genoa and Venice – would all have had their spies on the waterfront. If the Bristol merchants had stumbled on a bonanza they would have wanted to keep the secret to themselves for as long as possible. If they were importing cod from the Grand Banks without exchanging goods, the activity would not have been classified as 'trade' and therefore did not need not to be entered in the customs record, nor would duty have been payable.

It may be relevant that the city suffered no noticeable decline in its fortunes after the profitable trade with Iceland had been curtailed by the Hanseatic war. In fact, when the newly enthroned Henry VII visited the city he particularly noticed the conspicuous wealth of the people – this despite the protestations of the merchants that they were impoverished by the lack of trade with Iceland! Henry Tudor promptly demanded a contribution of £500 to the royal coffers and levied a tax of £1 on every man worth more than £200 *'because men's wives went so sumptuously apparelled'*.[10]

Opposite The Bristol Merchant, William Spencer (left of centre), is seen swearing in his successor as Lord Mayor of Bristol on 29 September 1479. Spencer was one of the financial backers of the 'Brasil' voyages from Bristol in the 1480s, when fishermen from Bristol probably succeeded in fishing off the coast of Newfoundland for cod, or 'stockfish'.

Above Master W's Kraeck (or carrack) c.1470, is one of the best-known medieval ship illustrations. The carrack was bigger than earlier ships with the castles fully integrated with the hull; the ship has a stern rudder and is carvel- or skeleton-built. Three substantial masts carry a variety of sails making the ship top heavy and fairly unstable by modern standards.

Windage was also a problem and the ship would have only modest sailing qualities.

In 1490 the English and the Hanseatic League settled their differences, and the peace treaty allowed the Bristolians to resume their previous trade with Iceland. Yet the merchants chose not to do so. Could this be because they were now settled into exploiting a much more lucrative source of stockfish elsewhere? It is frustrating, but no archaeological evidence that Bristol fishermen actually landed in Newfoundland prior to the sixteenth century has survived, but in the circumstances this is not surprising. Any huts or fish-drying racks that the fishermen might have constructed would have been built of timber and would not have endured the ravages of time. Fire, rot and later generations of fishermen would have combined to make it very unlikely that any physical evidence survived the intervening five centuries. But surprisingly, there is a written record which seems to confirm that the Bristolians were fishing off the coast of Newfoundland many years before either Cabot or Columbus crossed the Atlantic.

This final, crucial piece of the jigsaw comes from a letter written by the Englishman John Day to Christopher Columbus. This letter (which is given in full in Appendix 2.6) was only unearthed in the Spanish archives in 1955 and was written after John Cabot's successful voyage to Newfoundland in 1497. The critical passage reads:

> It is considered certain that the cape of the said land [found by Cabot in
> 1497] was found and discovered in the past by the men from Bristol who
> found 'Brasil' as your Lordship well knows. It was called the Island of Brasil,
> and it is assumed and believed to be the mainland that the men from Bristol
> found.[11]

Two things in the letter are significant. First is the confident tone of Day's statements: *'It is considered certain'* and *'as your Lordship well knows'*. This implies that knowledge of the discovery of Newfoundland was known and accepted by Columbus (and therefore presumably by many others as well) prior to Cabot's voyage of 1497. The second important element is the translation of the words *'in the past'*. The Spanish phrase *'en otros tiempos'* is normally used in the sense of 'about a generation ago', or twenty or thirty years.

This is the final and most convincing argument that the Bristol merchants were indeed sending ships to the Newfoundland area many years – perhaps even decades – before Columbus sailed to the Caribbean. It seems quite possible that the legacy of the trans-Atlantic voyages of St Brendan, and of Eirik, Leif and Bjarni to far-off Markland and Vinland, had been passed on by sailors trading in Iceland. Certainly the Norse sagas, with their stories of lush pastureland and rich fishing, had been written down for hundreds of years. English pirates and Basque whalers too would have retailed their drunken gossip in the harbour-side taverns of Europe.

The mid- to late fifteenth century saw the beginning of one of the world's great periods of global exploration. The explorer–mariners who set sail from Spain, Portugal and England were voyaging into an uncertain world over an ocean they called the Sea of Darkness, and in their remarkable exploits they were the astronauts of the day. But ships and crews were too valuable to waste on random exploration, and it is clear that these voyages were part of a systematic search for new trade routes or fishing grounds and that they were usually undertaken with a clear destination in mind.

Chance certainly played a part and some discoveries were fortuitous, but overall the discoveries that were made in the late fifteenth and early sixteenth centuries by Columbus, Cabot and their contemporaries were the outcome of good planning and competent organization. The success of every voyage depended on information brought back by previous expeditions and, in turn, each made its contribution to the late medieval understanding of the wider world beyond Europe.

CHAPTER 6

SLOW BOAT TO CHINA

The next thing that happened to them
was in a narrow part of the sea,
which was so entirely full of fishes
that the boat could go on no farther …

EDWARD LEAR *The Story of the Four Little Children*
Who Went Around the World

In the spring of 1955 an important letter was found in the Spanish archives at Simancas, a small medieval town in central Spain (see also p104). It is probably the most significant piece of evidence about the discovery of America to have turned up in the twentieth century and it has revolutionized our understanding of Cabot's voyages. Remarkably, it was discovered only by chance when an American language professor stumbled upon a document in the archives that referred to English voyages to the Americas. He mentioned his find to a fellow researcher, Dr Louis André Vigneras, who had already spent many years researching early voyages to America. When Vigneras finally located the document it became clear why the file had been overlooked for so long – the cover referred to an English voyage to Brazil, whereas the contents in fact concerned a passage to 'Brasil', the mythical island sought by the Bristol fishermen in the 1480s.

The document is a letter, handwritten in Spanish; it is well preserved and quite legible. It was written by John Day, an English spy who lived in Bristol, and was sent to a Spanish 'Grand Admiral', who historians now accept was Christopher Columbus.

A crew member from the BBC1 television series. John Cabot probably sailed with a crew of nineteen, including a Genoese barber and a friend from Burgundy. The rest were mostly local from Bristol, tough and probably illiterate. On both of his voyages in 1496 and 1497, the crew are reported to have 'confused him', or mutinied.

The letter (a full translation is given in Appendix 2.6) was almost certainly written between mid-December 1497 and mid-March 1498, and it tells us more about Cabot's voyage than any other single document. With the information it provides we can now piece together a picture of John Cabot and his movements after he left Valencia and went with his family to England.

⊚⊚⊚⊚⊚⊚⊚

When Cabot arrived in Bristol in late 1494 or early 1495 he had little time to lose, for it was clear that the Spanish meant business. Columbus had already left on his second trans-Atlantic voyage in September 1493 with seventeen vessels and a crew of 1200 to 1500 men. Columbus's flagship had a huge cabin, as befitted his new rank of Grand Admiral, and may have been as big as 200 tons. His instructions were to convert the local natives to Christianity (that would keep the Pope happy) and to establish a crown trading colony. In the spring of 1494 he revisited Cuba and convinced himself that the island was a peninsula of the mainland he sought. When Columbus returned to Spain later that year it was generally accepted that the Orient had at last been found – or at least that the Grand Admiral was adamant it had been. If Cabot was to mount an alternative voyage to Asia by a northern route he had to move fast!

Cabot had been turned down by both Spain and Portugal, so the logical place to go was England, the other contender in the search for routes across the Atlantic. Bristol had some of the most experienced Atlantic sailors in Europe and the port was ideally positioned. And like most other major European ports, it had a Genoese community who would give him the support he needed to establish himself.

Even though Bristolian sailors were highly experienced, Cabot would have cut an impressive figure in the city. It is unlikely that anyone else there had travelled as extensively or as far east as Alexandria and Mecca. He would have felt in his element, for these Atlantic ports also attracted the best shipbuilders and the finest construction materials that money could buy. The gossip was exciting and opportunities were unlimited. The three-masted caravel – the most popular ocean sailing ship of the period – was the interplanetary explorer of the early Renaissance. Given enough time, and with the inevitable loss of life from starvation, disease and accident among the crew, these tiny wooden ships could now sail almost anywhere in the known world – and beyond!

Cabot did his homework in Bristol before travelling to see the king and prepared carefully for his royal audience. He felt confident that Columbus had not reached the Orient proper, and one of several revelations in Day's letter suggests that it was common knowledge that Bristol fishermen had already sailed to North America (see quote p104).

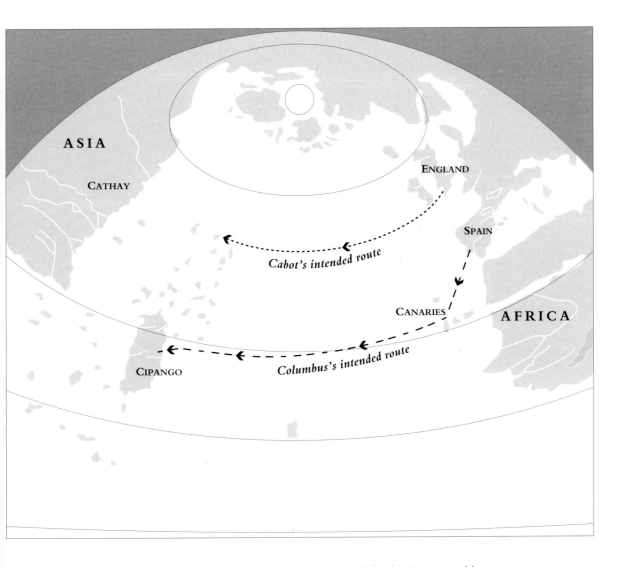

The approximate routes taken across the Atlantic by Columbus in 1492 and by
Cabot in 1497, superimposed on a map of the known world at that time (based on a
globe by Martin Behaim, 1492). When Columbus landed in the Caribbean, he was
convinced that he had found the offshore islands of the Orient. Cabot chose a more
northerly route, knowing that the distance would be shorter.

Soon he was in London making his presentation to King Henry VII: Columbus
had not found Cipango (Japan or Cathay), despite his claims, and land had already
been discovered by Bristol fishermen in the 1480s to the west of Bristol. Using maps
or a globe (most likely made by himself), Cabot explained why a northern route to
Asia would be shorter; once there, he would follow the coast, and if – as he predicted
– its trend was to the southwest he would eventually arrive in the land of the Great

HENRICVS,   VII ,

Khan. He would then be in the tropical latitudes that Columbus had reached but much farther to the west, in regions unexplored by Europeans.

A monarch gave royal authority for expeditions like these through letters patent. For a major new undertaking of the kind Cabot was proposing, which involved both economic and foreign policy, the implications were given the most careful consideration. Henry VII was no 'rubber-stamp' monarch but a king who took an active part in the running of his country. Then, once the decision had been made, there was the lengthy process of drawing up a legal document, every word and phrase of which would have been scrutinized and weighed. Eventually, on 5 March 1496, Henry VII granted letters patent to John Cabot. The original is written in Latin, but a modern English translation reads:

> Be it known and made manifest that we have given and granted ... to our
> well-beloved John Cabot, citizen of Venice, and to Lewis, Sebastian and Sancio,
> sons of the said John, and to their heirs ... full and free authority ... to sail
> to all parts, regions and coasts of the eastern, western and northern sea ...[1]

Henry VII had received a similar proposal in 1488–89 from Bartholomew Columbus on behalf of his brother Christopher. However, whether through prevarication or because he turned him down flat, Henry missed the opportunity to act as royal sponsor for the greatest expedition of the age, and he was not going to make the same mistake a second time. But he had to be careful. Spain and Portugal were making discoveries throughout the Atlantic and only two years earlier the Pope had issued a papal decree, the Treaty of Tordesillas, that divided up the New World between the two Iberian states. So Henry was circumspect in the wording of his letters patent to Cabot, granting leave to sail only to the east, west and north; he was careful not to give Cabot permission to sail south since that could lead to encroachment on land already claimed by the other two countries. The English king did not want a territorial dispute with either Portugal or Spain.

ᘒᘒᘒᘒᘒᘒᘒᘒ

Henry Tudor (1457-1509) was the first ruler of the house of Tudor.
He defeated Richard III at Bosworth Field in 1485 and was subsequently
crowned Henry VII of England. His reign initiated a period of national unity
following the strife of the fifteenth century. The early years of Henry's life had been
spent in conditions of adversity, usually in poverty and often in danger. Thus Henry
grew up to be secretive and cautious, with a reputation for being parsimonious.
He was also an avaricious man and Henry supported Cabot's voyages in 1496,
1497 and 1498, although his financial backing was limited. He died 21 April
1509, and was succeeded by his second son, Henry VIII.

Cabot wasted no time in returning to Bristol and set about preparing for the coming voyage. But he might have been a little too impatient; one revelation made in Day's letter is that the 1497 expedition was not his first. In the early summer of 1496 Cabot had set out from Bristol on a voyage that was not known of before the document's discovery. He may have used a ship that was not suitable for the purpose – or possibly he took the newly-completed *Matthew,* untried and untested. Whatever his intentions on that occasion, we know from Day's letter that the attempt was a failure:

> Since your Lordship wants information relating to the first voyage, here is what happened: he went with one ship, his crew confused him, he was short of supplies and ran into bad weather, and he decided to turn back.[2]

Cabot sailed ill-prepared and had serious problems with his crew – the comment that they '*confused him*' may indicate that there was a mutiny of some kind. It is even possible that he unknowingly took Spanish spies on board whose mission was to make sure that the voyage was aborted. Ports were riddled with spies and informers, and John Day (whose real name was Hugh Say) himself is thought to have been a double-agent, so England's rivals were kept well informed of these voyages from Bristol. Henry had already received a delegation from the Portuguese king asking him to refrain from supporting a voyage across the Atlantic Ocean. Neither the Spanish nor the Portuguese were prepared to make room for a third member of their exclusive trans-Atlantic club.

Cabot and his family spent the winter of 1496–7 in Bristol preparing for the next voyage. From his rent book we know that they lived in St Nicholas Street and paid forty shillings (£2) in annual rent. This was a relatively high rent for the time, so the house would have been quite large – though Cabot was not wealthy at this time.

Although the king had given permission for the voyage he did not finance the project, so Cabot looked for financial backing in Bristol. It was common practice for the city's merchants to club together to support ventures such as his, thereby spreading both the risk and the profit. However, since he took only one ship in 1496 and 1497 (despite having royal assent for up to five), it appears that Cabot met with limited interest from his prospective backers.

☙☙☙☙☙☙☙

We know little about the origins of the *Matthew.* The Bristol customs records for between 1493 and 1503 are missing. No ship of that name is listed in the records for 1492–93, but the accounts kept from 1503–04 list a 'bark' called the *Matthew* that sailed between Ireland, Bristol and Bordeaux. On the basis of this scanty evidence we

CHARTS

The use of maritime charts was still in its infancy when Cabot sailed to Newfoundland, although the very earliest chart, known as the *Carta Pisana,* was drawn by Italian and Catalan pilots as early as 1275. William Caxton brought the first printing press to London only in 1476, so in Cabot's day charts and sailing instructions were still produced by hand.

It has been said that English sailors were unaccustomed to the use of charts until Cabot came to Bristol and introduced the concept from the Mediterranean, but the sailors of Bristol certainly kept notes as a guide to navigation that gave both a course and a distance to sail. Some sailing directions were considered too valuable to be allowed to fall into unfriendly hands – the Portuguese introduced the death penalty for revealing information acquired during their voyages around Africa.

One of the most prized possessions of a mariner was the pilot-book or *rutter,* a small pocket-book in which navigational information was recorded, including magnetic courses and distances between ports and capes, the direction and flow of tidal currents, the times of high water at new and full moon at important ports, details of headlands and channels, the nature of the sea bed, soundings and even changes in the colour of the water. The oldest English rutter dates from the early fifteenth century and gives sailing directions for the circumnavigation of England and a voyage to the Strait of Gibraltar. An early rutter from Bristol gives directions on how to return from Spain: '… *at capfenister* [Cape Finisterre] *go your cours north north est. And ye gesse you ij parties ovir the see and be bound into sebarne* [the Severn Estuary] *ye must north and by est till ye come into Sowdying* [the soundings, or 100-fathom line].'[4]

Cabot would have used these rutters. A skilled cartographer, he would also have drawn his own charts, although none have survived. When he returned from Newfoundland in 1497 and visited the king to report on his discoveries, he took as a visual aid a globe which he had constructed himself, probably of parchment-covered wood.

❧❧❧❧❧❧❧❧❧❧❧

can only assume that the *Matthew* was a relatively new ship, probably built in Bristol for the 1497 voyage. Cabot had learnt his lessons after the abortive attempt of 1496 and made a better job of preparing for the new expedition.

However, the records kept for other ships of the period give us a good idea of how the ship was provisioned. Cabot would have taken food for, probably, six months and water for three. The crew's diet would have been unappetizing, basic and bulky and may well have started to rot even before the ship was out of the Bristol Channel. The staple food was boring: salt meat, salt or smoked fish and bread, washed down with beer which kept better than plain water.

Overleaf A modern interpretation of the departure of the *Matthew* in 1497. John Cabot and his middle son, Sebastian, look on as the ship is prepared for the voyage. In the background is St Mary's, Redcliffe, which Queen Elizabeth I claimed was the fairest parish church in the whole of her kingdom. The church is shown without a spire, which was destroyed during an electrical storm in 1446 and had not been re-built by 1497.

Loading for a long voyage took several weeks, with everything noted carefully in the purser's book of daily expenses. In preparation for a sailing in May large quantities of dried stockfish would have been brought down in barrels as early as March – stockfish keeps for a year and so could be loaded early. By mid-April a couple of oxen would have been killed and salted down in barrels. Bread was bought in huge quantities; some – probably a type of ship's biscuit or hardtack – was also loaded early. Plenty of flour was also taken so that fresh bread could be made; this was baked in an open hearth or even an oven – at least during settled weather. Beer was loaded in huge quantities with a daily allowance of at least a gallon per man.

Shortly before departure live animals arrived, with their fodder; a cow (medieval breeds were smaller than today's) or a couple of goats would give fresh milk and, one day, fresh meat. Chickens provided eggs before also ending up in the pot. If the crew were lucky a few small luxuries might find their way on board before departure: perhaps some vegetables, honey and salted butter.

The number of meals that sailors ate was regulated by the *Rolls of Oléron* – a medieval rule book that set out the rights and duties of English sailors.[3] This defined the role of the vessel's master and gives us an insight into the way Cabot was required by law to behave. He was to maintain discipline and had the right to mete out severe punishment, but he was also bound by majority decisions of the crew. If the master enforced his own wish against such a decision he was held personally responsible for any unfavourable consequences. In the case of jettison of cargo, a third of the ship's company had to agree that it was necessary before it could go ahead. In the event of serious misdemeanours, such as mayhem, robbery or homicide, as many as possible of the fellow-mariners of the accused would be summoned and a verdict passed by majority vote. If the guilty sailor had inflicted a serious wound, he paid damages of 100 shillings (£5); if he had killed a man he was hanged.

@@@@@@@@

Typically, a vessel of the *Matthew*'s size would carry a master, master's mate, priest, steward, boatswain, cook, carpenter, cooper and possibly a gunner and a soldier. We know from historical records that Cabot also took a Burgundian (a friend) and a Genoese barber – partly because the fashion of the day was to be clean-shaven, but surely also for the luxury of conversation in his native tongue. The rest were mostly from Bristol, as Raimondo de Soncino indicated in a letter to the Duke of Milan:

> This Messer Zoane, as a foreigner and a poor man, would not have obtained credence, had it not been that his companions, who are practically all English and from Bristol, testified that he spoke the truth.[5]

NAVIGATION

Cabot would have envied the modern electronic navigational equipment available on the new *Matthew,* which, day or night, can give the ship's position anywhere in the world to an accuracy of better than a hundred metres. By comparison, fifteenth-century navigation was much more of an art.

Central to Cabot's aids to navigation was a rudimenary *compass,* which allowed the helmsman to hold a reasonably accurate course. The compass was divided into 32 'points', each of eleven and a quarter degrees. At best it was an uncertain instrument, with a needle that swung wildly in rough weather. Nor was the deviation in the earth's magnetic field fully understood, and this would have caused changes of several degrees during a passage across the Atlantic.

Cabot's crew would have had to estimate their speed through the water as the technique of measuring the speed of a ship with a *log* – literally a log at the end of a knotted length of rope – was not invented until around 1575. (The term 'knots' is still used today as a measure of the speed of a ship or aircraft.) The course and estimated speed of a ship were recorded every half-hour – the time period was measured using a *sand-glass,* which was religiously turned every thirty minutes by a ship's boy. These half-hourly measurements were recorded on a wooden *traverse board,* which had eight holes drilled along each of the primary compass points, each hole corresponding to a half-hourly course reading. Without an accurate clock a navigator cannot calculate his longitude, so these half-hourly measurements were the only way of calculating distance sailed in an east–west direction, a technique known as 'dead-reckoning'.

Cabot would have been able to measure his latitude (his position relative to the Pole or Equator) using a *cross-staff* or *astrolabe.* The astrolabe was more accurate but was difficult to use on a rolling ship. By referring to simple declination tables, either instrument could be used to measure latitude from the sun or the Pole Star – if the skies were clear.

When close to shore, a crewman would use a *sounding-line* or *lead-line* to measure the depth of water. Other skills used by these early mariners included noting the direction in which land-birds flew in the hope that this would show where over the horizon land might lie – a tradition that goes back at least as far as Noah! Even today, trained Polynesian navigators are so sensitive to patterns in the ocean waves that they can detect the presence of islands downwind from the subtle changes caused by reflection. No doubt John Cabot and his contemporaries benefited from a wide variety of intuitive skills which are now lost to sailors today who depend on diesel engines, reliable charts and satellite navigation.

Cabot sailed with between eighteen and twenty crew and, most likely, one other humble but indispensable member of a ship's complement: the ship's cat. A famous law introduced by Edward I in 1275 stated that if any living thing, be it a man, dog or cat, escaped from a stricken vessel, then it was no wreck – a provision which partly explains why ship's cats were so common. But these ships also swarmed with rats and other vermin, making a skilful cat an essential member of the crew.

The various records differ on the date of sailing, although all are in agreement on the date that Cabot arrived in North America. According to the Fust document, a sixteenth-century manuscript that was destroyed by fire in the last century, Cabot left Bristol on 2 May 1497, made landfall on 24 June and returned to Bristol on 6 August.[6] John Day, in his letter to Columbus, implied a different date for the departure:

> They left England toward the end of May, and must have been on the way
> 35 days before sighting land.[7]

If the estimate of '*35 days*' is correct, working back from 24 June suggests that Cabot departed on 20 May. Another observer, Lorenzo Pasqualigo, noted that Cabot was '*three months on the voyage*';[8] taken at face value, this gives a starting date of 8 May.

These discrepancies may simply be due to differences of opinion on what constituted 'departure'. It would have taken one, or perhaps two, tides for the *Matthew* to be towed down the River Avon by tenders rowed by a team of men. Once in the Bristol Channel, she would have stayed at anchor in King Road until a favourable wind allowed her to sail west towards the open ocean. The prevailing direction was from the west and the southwest – and medieval ships could not sail closer than at right-angles to the wind. So it would have been normal to lie in King Road until a wind with an easterly component began to blow, and a wait of several weeks would not have been unusual.

Once a favourable wind set in the *Matthew* and all the other ships – perhaps dozens by the end of a long wait – would have been off together, making for the open ocean as quickly as possible. No sailor feels comfortable close to shore, and Cabot would have used the fierce tides in the Bristol Channel to his advantage. Spring tides there run faster than the *Matthew* could sail, so if the winds were light he probably anchored for six hours during the flood and waited for the ebb to sweep the ship westwards once again – literally flushing her into the open ocean. He might also have put into harbour in South Wales or southern Ireland to top up the water casks and take on fresh food. This would only be seamanlike with a voyage of uncertain duration ahead.

The unavoidable delays in putting to sea and the option of putting into port somewhere on the way could well account for the different dates suggested for Cabot's departure. When David Allan-Williams sets out in the new *Matthew* in 1997 he will face exactly the same problems of tide and wind, and in all probability he too will take the opportunity to put into harbour somewhere in Wales or Ireland before finally committing his vessel and its crew to the uncertainties of the North Atlantic.

❀❀❀❀❀❀❀

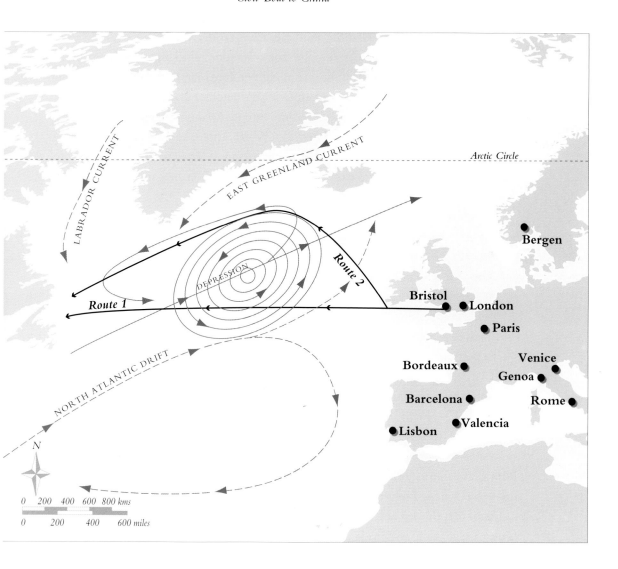

What route did Cabot take? The historic evidence of Cabot's 1497 route
is inconclusive. The ship would have been subjected to two natural forces,
current and wind. If Cabot had sailed a direct route (Route 1) to Newfoundland,
he would have battled against the North Atlantic Drift. The prevailing winds are also
from the west and southwest – a function of depressions which sweep eastwards across
the Atlantic. Combined, they would make westwards progress for a fifteenth-century
caravel practically impossible. His alternative route would be to sail northwest initially
(Route 2). Once north of about 60°N and north of the depression track,
Cabot would experience favourable easterly and northeasterly winds. He would also
have unknowingly benefited from the favourable East Greenland and
Labrador currents.

Unlike Columbus, who sailed the southerly route to the Caribbean with the warm trade winds blowing from behind, Cabot took the more challenging northern route. Not only was he sailing against the prevailing winds, which blow from the west and southwest in a constant series of atmospheric depressions, but he would also have battled against the remnants of the Gulf Stream. In mid-Atlantic this becomes the North Atlantic Drift and flows at up to a knot from North America to Europe – though this would not have been known to fifteenth-century sailors. The current would have significantly slowed the progress of a medieval ship, which at best might average only four knots sailing into the wind.

There are two main sources of information about Cabot's crossing, although some of the details given could be misleading. John Day wrote:

> They left England toward the end of May, and must have been on the way
> 35 days before sighting land; the wind was east-north-east and the sea calm
> going and coming back, except for one day when he ran into a storm two or
> three days before finding land; and going so far out, his compass needle failed
> to point north and marked two rhumbs below.[9]

A northeasterly wind that continued for over a month would have been a rare occurrence in the North Atlantic. The evidence for climatic conditions in the 1490s suggests that weather conditions in England were unsettled, with a series of depressions moving across the country bringing *westerly* winds. Cabot returned from Newfoundland in just fifteen days – a remarkably fast passage, averaging five knots, for a ship whose bottom would have been fouled by marine growth and one that indicates that this leg at least was made before a following, westerly wind. If the outward passage really was made with the benefit of an easterly wind, as Day suggests, it is unlikely that the voyage would have lasted as long as thirty-five days unless the wind was very light.

Raimondo de Soncino gives a pointer to another possibility:

> 'He started from Bristol, a port on the west of this kingdom, passed Ireland,
> which is still further west, and then bore towards the north, in order to sail to
> the east, leaving the north [i.e. Pole Star] on his right hand after some days. After
> having wandered for some time he at length arrived at the mainland …'[10]

This is a more convincing account of Cabot's crossing. Soncino writes that he '*wandered for some time*' – suggesting that the ship had to tack into the more usual westerly winds, against which the *Matthew* would have made little progress. Having left Dursey

Head in Ireland behind him and with the open North Atlantic ahead, Cabot may have sailed northwest towards a position southwest of Iceland (a route that was very familiar to Bristol fishermen). This would eventually have led him north of the track of the Atlantic depressions where the ship would have experienced more favourable easterly winds. It could be that this is what Day alludes to in his letter but – whether through ignorance or brevity – without mentioning that Cabot initially sailed north before encountering winds from the east-northeast.

A route this far north would certainly have been much colder, but the *Matthew*'s crew were well used to sailing to Iceland and beyond. The unhappiest people on board were probably Cabot and his barber, both more used to the balmy conditions of the Mediterranean. Interestingly, none of the contemporary reports mentions either icebergs or dense fog, which they must have encountered on the voyage. However, when Cabot returned to make his report to the king he would have wanted to present a positive and encouraging account of the passage and so might deliberately have passed over some of the hazards that had been faced.

Life on board during the voyage would have been tough by today's standards. The food, basic and unappetizing at the best of times, would have begun to deteriorate. Dried and barrelled meats became riddled with maggots and worms,

CLIMATIC CHANGE

Climatic conditions during the late fifteenth century were not as benign as during the earlier Norse explorations. The period between the fourteenth and late nineteenth centuries is often referred to as the Little Ice Age, although this generally cooler period was interspersed with short periods of warmer weather. The 1430s were a cold decade when the River Thames in London froze six or eight times. But from the late 1430s to 1506 reports of the Thames freezing were much less frequent, indicating that conditions had become warmer. In the 1490s the summers were generally wetter, which suggests unsettled weather patterns over the Atlantic, with a series of depressions sweeping across the British Isles. With these conditions prevailing the western Atlantic (western Greenland and Labrador) would probably have been unusually cold, with large amounts of drift ice moving southwards from the Davis Strait.

the bread and flour rife with weevils and other creatures; even the water turned rancid during long ocean voyages. Parasitic infestation of food was such a problem that nearly everyone suffered from intestinal worms. Ferdinand Columbus gave a most graphic description of on-board cuisine during his father's fourth passage to the Caribbean islands:

'What with the heat and the dampness, our ship biscuit had become so wormy that, God help me, I saw many who waited for darkness to eat porridge made of it, that they might not see the maggots, and others were so used to eating them that they didn't even trouble to pick them out because they might lose their supper had they been so nice.'[11]

Except during the very worst weather the crew slept on deck, rolled in a blanket or a spare sail. During bad weather they would be forced below deck, where the air was fetid and space was shared with rotting food and the ship's colony of rats. Almost anything was preferable to sleeping in these conditions. At night the ship sailed in almost total darkness, the only candle casting a pale glow across the helmsman's steering compass. The crew were poor men, fortunate even to have a change of clothing. What they owned they wore; their coats were of coarse wool and their shirts of linen. Everything would be salty and would never fully dry out, even on the warmest of June days. Although the men had leather shoes they preferred to work barefoot, which gave them greater purchase on the wet, wooden decks. The other few possessions they owned, such as wooden bowls or a leather drinking mug, would be identified with a roughly scratched mark rather than their initials because most of these men could neither read nor write.

It is not certain, but a priest might have sailed on the *Matthew*. If so, he would have held a Latin Mass on deck for the crew every day. Everyone was Catholic and religion was deeply rooted in their daily lives. Work did not stop during Mass and crew members would not necessarily even take part except on Sundays. But, in an uncertain world, the very act of this religious worship happening in their midst would have been reassuring. Other distractions during a voyage included games of dice and backgammon.

Of the landing on 24 June 1497, St John the Baptist's Day, we know plenty. The Fust manuscript and the letters of Lorenzo Pasqualigo, Raimondo de Soncino and John Day all give broadly similar and complementary accounts. Cabot went ashore with a small party and took possession of the land on behalf of the king of England. They raised the banners of Henry VII, Pope Alexander VI and St Mark, the last *'as he is a Venetian'*,[12] and erected a crucifix on the foreshore. The crew followed a trail inland and discovered the remnants of a fire; they also found animal manure and a stick *'half a yard long pierced at both ends, carved and painted with brazil'*.[13] The climate was said to be temperate and tall trees grew *'of the kind masts are made'*.[14] But Cabot was nervous about being ashore with a small group and *'did not dare advance inland beyond the shooting distance of a cross-bow'*.[15] The crew filled their water casks and returned to the ship. This was the only time they went ashore, although they sailed along the coast and surveyed for another month before returning to England. Day also reported sightings of what appeared to be *'fields'* and of *'two forms running on land one after the other'*, but the ship was too far offshore to see if they were people or animals.[16]

Exactly where Cabot landed and his subsequent route have kept historians in hot debate for a century or more and the people of Newfoundland and Nova Scotia wax passionate about the landfall site. As we have seen, it is unlikely that Cabot sailed in a straight line from Ireland; more probably he zigzagged his way across the Atlantic, making the best headway he could against a predominantly westerly wind. Day remarks that Cabot had navigational problems: *'his compass needle failed to point north and marked two rhumbs* [22.5 degrees] *below'*;[17] today, magnetic deviation is well understood, but in Cabot's time there was little understanding of the phenomenon. During the voyage the sailors would have estimated the speed of the ship and kept a record of the distance travelled through the water. This, however, would not have made allowance for ocean currents, about which Cabot had little reliable information.

The distance sailed by Cabot varies according to the source: John Day reported that it was 1800 miles (he may have meant Spanish *millas* – 1800 *millas* is 1440 nautical miles); Pasqualigo gave it as 700 leagues (equal to 2226 nautical miles if this was the Italian league of 3.18 nautical miles used by Columbus); and Soncino recorded that Cabot *'found two very large and fertile new islands … 400 leagues from England'*.[19] But if Cabot did indeed steer a variable course across the Atlantic because of prevailing westerly winds these distances become meaningless anyway. Medieval sailors could not measure their longitude (their position in an east–west direction) because they had no way of keeping

SAILING A MEDIEVAL SHIP

Sailors of medieval times wanted the wind to be on the quarter or from behind. If the wind came from ahead (which they called 'scant') or less than five points (56 degrees) from the direction they wanted to go, they either dropped their sails and 'hove to' if the wind was too strong or they sailed as close as they could to it. This is called beating to windward – or 'traversing', as medieval sailors termed it. If the wind was 'scant' a medieval ship had to 'traverse' across the ocean, effectively tacking with the wind first on one side and then on the other.

In addition, a sailing boat always 'slips' sideways through the water, especially when sailing close to the wind; this sideways drift is called leeway and in a medieval ship could result in the true course being at least 20 degrees to the downwind side of the direction in which the ship was heading. In practice, therefore, medieval ships were unlikely to make a better course than approximately at right-angles to the wind direction. In 1583 Sir Humfry Gilbert sailed to Newfoundland on a due west course and encountered 'winde alwayes so scant' from the westerly quarter 'that our traverse was great'[18]. His ship zigzagged across the Atlantic, going as far south as latitude 41° and as far north as 51°; he eventually missed the harbour he wanted and ended up in northern Newfoundland.

◎◎◎◎◎◎◎◎◎

accurate time, but Cabot and his contemporaries could measure their latitude from the sun or Pole Star, which told them how far north or south they were. This allowed them to sail back to their preferred latitude if they were blown off course by adverse winds. Soncino records that Cabot sailed *'… to the east* [meaning the oriental East], *leaving the north* [star] *on his right hand after some days …'*[20].

Because of Cabot's inability to measure longitude and the unreliability of using speed to estimate the real distance travelled (called dead-reckoning – see the boxed article on 'Navigation', page 117), the most accurate way of calculating where he made landfall is to rely on the historically recorded information on his latitude. Using an astrolabe or a cross-staff, Cabot would have measured the angle the stars or the sun made with the horizon. The astrolabe was an accurate instrument but difficult to use in rough seas; the cross-staff was less accurate but easier to use. Because of these problems, some historians dismiss the latitudinal evidence and suggest that Cabot made his landfall south of Newfoundland in Nova Scotia or even Maine and that he discovered most of the 'New-Founde-Land' only after turning back for England. A southerly landing would certainly have been encouraged by the Labrador current, which would have set the ship south as it approached North America.

However, it would have been logical for Cabot to have measured his latitude on the one occasion that he landed (or when at anchor), and this would have given him a very precise fix. Even at sea it is likely that medieval navigators were better at measuring their latitude than we might suppose. In 1991 Sir Robin Knox-Johnston retraced the voyage of Columbus in his small yacht, *Suhali,* and plotted his course using only a medieval astrolabe. His *least* accurate fix was just 30 miles (48 kilometres) from his true position and several of his best fixes were only 5 miles (8 kilometres) out – which corresponds to the smallest increment that can be estimated on this simple instrument. Knox-Johnston's practical experiment with the astrolabe suggests that medieval navigators were able to determine their position at sea with greater precision than many historians have supposed, and the latitudes implied in John Day's letter therefore have a crucial role to play in determining Cabot's landing place:

> 'Thus your Lordship will know that the cape nearest to Ireland is 1800 miles west of Dursey Head which is in Ireland, and the southernmost part of the Island of the Seven Cities is west of Bordeaux River …'[21]

Dursey Head (lat. 51°34′N) is on roughly the same latitude as Cape Bauld, the most northerly tip of Newfoundland and close to the site where the Norse established their settlement at L'Anse-aux-Meadows. Day's other reference is to the southern tip of the Island of the Seven Cities, which *'is west of Bordeaux River'*. Today, the river – whose mouth lies at latitude 45°35′N – is called the Gironde; this latitude is only a few miles south of Cape Breton Island.

The other evidence for the location of Cabot's landfall is the information we are given about his subsequent 'coasting'. Pasqualigo reports that Cabot coasted for 300

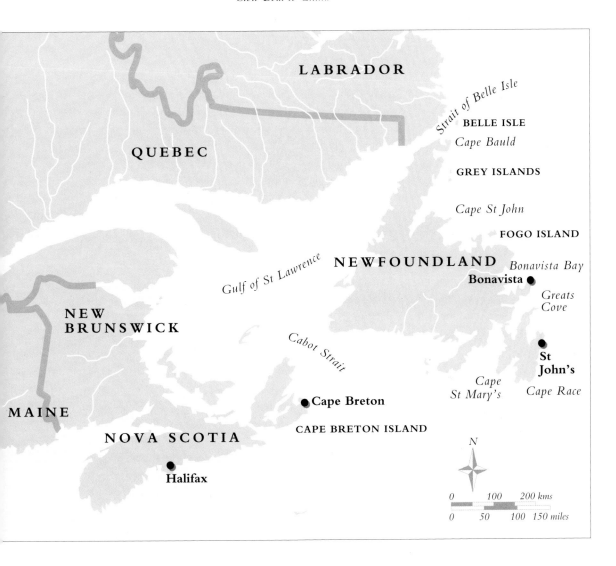

The site of Cabot's only landing in North America has caused much controversy,
but there are essentially five main options:
(1) near Cape Breton, then he sailed southwest along the shore of Nova Scotia;
(2) in Nova Scotia, then sailed back to the northeast along the south coast
of Newfoundland;
(3) into the Gulf of St Lawrence, then returning via the south coast of Newfoundland;
(4) in northern Newfoundland near Cape Bauld, then down the east coast of
Newfoundland before retracing his route north;
(5) in northern Newfoundland near Cape Bauld, through the Strait of Belle Isle into
the Gulf of St Lawrence and around Newfoundland.

THE MCCARTHY DIARY

Jack Dodd, a Newfoundland sea captain who died in the 1980s, owned a goatskin-covered diary which he claimed contained details of Cabot's voyage of 1497. The diary was supposed to have been written by an Irishman called Daniel McCarthy who helped Cabot to prepare for his voyage. However, before the ship's departure McCarthy's father died in Dublin, so he returned to take over the family's cooperage business. McCarthy asked another member of the crew, a man called O'Driscoll, to keep a log of the voyage, and it is this record which was incorporated into McCarthy's personal diary. The diary perished in a house fire in the 1940s and it is now impossible to establish its authenticity. Fortunately, Jack Dodd knew the contents by heart and wrote down the details from memory.

Some of the information in the reconstructed diary directly contradicts the established historical record, while other parts are complementary. For example, the diary states, correctly, that Cabot was born in Genoa but goes on to claim that he entered a monastery in Venice, where he befriended an older monk called Anthony Matthew. The diary also maintains that Cabot knew little about sailing and relied on the experience of others.

In Bristol, he is said to have acquired a ship called the *Sea Hawk,* which he renamed the *Matthew* in honour of his friend in Venice. The ship was about eighty feet (24 metres) long and had a displacement of 120 tons. The provisions for the voyage are described in great detail: salted and dried beef, pork, fish, goat meat, mutton, dried rice, beans, meal flour, cheese and jams; and the livestock taken on board included ten goats, ten sheep, two cows three mules, forty hens and ducks and six pigs – all requiring vast quantities of fodder. Twenty-seven men are said to have sailed, including many Irishmen and two monks – but no Burgundian.

The diary gives a day-by-day account of the voyage, during which there were several storms. Apparently, the *Matthew* could average ten knots in light winds – an unlikely speed for a ship of her type. She left Bristol on 17 May 1497 and land was sighted on 24 June; a landing was made at a place called Flatrock near St John's, Newfoundland.

It is claimed that Cabot met Beothuk Indians and that the crew even lived with them for a time. The Beothuk had with them black Newfoundland dogs (a domesticated breed that was not recognized until several hundred years later). According to the diary Cabot also had enough live animals left to present the Indians with a horse, two goats, two sheep and several chickens – although it is unlikely that these animals could have been kept alive on board for all this time.

Perhaps the most telling anachronism is seen in the list of food taken on board in Bristol, which included 'Indian meal flour', molasses and potatoes – none of which was introduced to Europe until the sixteenth century. The real tragedy is that the original diary no longer exists: although the version reconstructed by Dodd certainly contains many fanciful references, the original may well have contained valuable information that is now lost to us.

A medieval crew like that aboard the *Matthew* would have worked, eaten and slept on deck and only went below during the very worst conditions. The heavy labour required to sail a medieval ship meant these men were immensely strong and their daily diet comprised nearly 6,000 calories – twice that of an average man today. Scurvy, resulting from a lack of Vitamin C, became a serious problem once these long ocean voyages began to be made during the late fifteenth century.

leagues (about 780 nautical miles); Soncino, that he found two very large and fertile islands; and Day asserts that most of the land was discovered *after* the ship had turned back. So where exactly did Cabot land?

Historians disagree over the site of Cabot's landfall and estimates vary from as far north as Labrador to as far south as Florida, but most agree it is likely to be in Newfoundland, Nova Scotia or even Maine. Some historians have argued that Cabot made his landfall near Cape Breton and then sailed southwest along the coast of Nova Scotia; others that he landed in Nova Scotia and coasted back to the northeast, past Cape Breton and to the southern coast of Newfoundland. A third theory is that he sailed past Cape Breton into the Gulf of St Lawrence, then turned around and sailed back along the southern coast of Newfoundland.

Those who rely on the accuracy of the latitudinal information put Cabot's landfall in northern Newfoundland near Cape Bauld, and here there are two options – either he then sailed down the eastern side of the island, or he passed through the Strait of Belle Isle and into the Gulf of St Lawrence, continuing on around Newfoundland to exit along the southern coast. However, the Strait of Belle Isle is usually blocked by drift ice until July. If anything, ice conditions in 1497 would have made a passage by a sailing ship even more difficult than it is today, and no experienced mariner would put his vessel at risk in sea ice. So a passage anticlockwise around Newfoundland is the less likely option.

If Cabot did make landfall near Cape Bauld, it is likely that he then proceeded down the east coast of Newfoundland, perhaps sailing offshore from one headland to another. Once the southeastern tip of the island had been rounded he would have seen open water stretching out to the west. He may then have turned back and, closing the shore, made a closer inspection of the island, surveying as he went. This would account for Day's statement that *'most of the land was discovered after turning back'*.

On 24 June 1997 the new *Matthew* will make its landfall at Bonavista near the eastern end of the island, a site that has been a Newfoundland favourite at least as far back as a map published in 1617. However, it is unlikely to have been the original landfall. When the 400th anniversary was celebrated in 1897 Bonavista was a convenient location, accessible by dignitaries from St John's, and a statue was erected. So, although a landing by John Cabot at Cape Bonavista is historically improbable, the 500th anniversary celebrations will continue to honour the tradition.

ⓔⓔⓔⓔⓔⓔⓔ

Cabot left North America towards the end of July 1497, having coasted for a month. All the contemporary writers mention the vast quantities of cod. Soncino reported:

'They assert that the sea there is swarming with fish, which can be taken not only with the net, but in baskets let down with a stone, so that it sinks in the water. I have heard this Messer Zoane state so much.'[22]

Day wrote:

'All along the coast they found many fish like those which in Iceland are dried in the open and sold in England and other countries ...'[24]

The *Matthew* made her very fast return to Europe in just fifteen days. Such a rapid passage (at an average speed of 5 knots) could only have been made with a westerly wind blowing from behind and, as suggested earlier, throws into question Day's claim that Cabot sailed a direct route to North America with a constant east-northeast wind blowing for 35 days.

But Cabot's troubles were not over. According to John Day:

'... they returned to the coast of Europe in fifteen days. They had the wind behind them, and he reached Brittany because the sailors confused him, saying that he was heading too far north. From there he came to Bristol, and he went to see the King to report to him all the above mentioned ...'[24]

As during his first attempt in 1496, there was dissent on Cabot's ship and *'the sailors confused him'*. He arrived back in Bristol on 6 August, no doubt a happy and relieved man and very much a local celebrity. Almost immediately, he left for London to see Henry VII with a much grander plan in mind.

CHAPTER 7

THE FINAL VOYAGE

And off they sailed among the waves,
Far and far away:
They sailed across the silent main,
And reached the great Gromboolian Plain;
And there they play forevermore
At battlecock and shuttledore.

EDWARD LEAR *The Daddy Long-legs and the Fly*

When John Cabot returned from his successful voyage to North America in August 1497 he rode straight to London to see the king. Today you can drive the 120 miles (190 kilometres) between Bristol and the capital in less than two and a half hours, but in Cabot's day the roads were rough and often muddy and the journey probably took him three days. He would have travelled with companions for safety because robbers and brigands frequently lay in wait for the hapless traveller. Cabot returned from his voyage on 6 August and the household books of King Henry VII show that he was granted an audience with the king on 10 August, so it would appear that he wasted little time in cashing in on his success.

Within two weeks the first reports of Cabot's achievement were on their way to foreign countries. These letters (a selection of which are given in Appendix 2) were mainly from ambassadors to the court of Henry VII and they tell us most of what we know about Cabot and his voyage. We know he made a presentation and that he used a globe to explain his voyage more clearly. The Duke of Milan's ambassador, Raimondo de Soncino, wrote:

Cabot sailed from Bristol for the last time in early May 1498, but what happened to him and his fleet of five ships is still a mystery. Did he return quietly to England having failed, a broken and destitute man? Or did he and his ships perish during the crossing leaving no trace? Or is there another explanation: did Cabot and some of his ships succeed in crossing the North Atlantic a second time, only to die by other, more sinister, means?

131

> This Messer Zoane has the description of the world in a map, and also
> in a solid sphere, which he has made, and shows where he has been ...
> He tells all this in such a way, and makes everything so plain, that I also feel
> compelled to believe him.[1]

It was a critical time for Cabot. If he was going to capitalize on his success he had to
be very persuasive before the king. His first attempt to cross the Atlantic in 1496 had
failed and he could not risk anyone doubting the success of the voyage he had just
completed. What he wanted was backing for a full expeditionary fleet the following
year, in 1498. He was now a national hero and could take advantage of his sudden
fame. Lorenzo Pasqualigo, writing to his brothers in Venice on 23 August, noted that
Cabot was *'called the Great Admiral and vast honour is paid to him and he goes dressed in
silk, and these English run after him like mad ...'*[2]

   Henry VII had been wary of investing in Cabot's original proposals. But after the
second voyage the king saw the opportunity to build on its success and expand
English influence westwards across the Atlantic. At first everyone seemed to have got
a little carried away with enthusiasm for the next project and the promises were very
grand indeed. In his letter Pasqualigo reported:

> The king has promised him for the spring ten armed ships as he [Cabot]
> desires ...[3]

Raimondo de Soncino wrote to the Duke of Milan:

> This next spring his Majesty means to send him with fifteen or twenty
> ships.[4]

The king was certainly pleased with Cabot and granted him an annual pension of
twenty pounds – a sum that is confirmed in an accounts roll from the Bristol customs.[5] The pension was not overly generous, but it was a token of the king's gratitude.
It was to be paid to Cabot not direct from the royal coffers but from income raised
from Bristol customs – typical of the canny and parsimonious king!

   In due course Henry issued Cabot new letters patent on 3 February 1498 giving
him the right to explore the Atlantic for new territories.[6] The king now had high
hopes for this new venture and was prepared to tentatively challenge the Spanish.
Pedro de Ayala, at the time a junior ambassador at the court of England, wrote to
King Ferdinand and Queen Isabella about the new voyage:

Having seen the course they are steering and the length of the voyage, I
find that what they have discovered or are in search of is possessed by Your
Highnesses … by the convention with Portugal [i.e. the Treaty of Tordesillas].
It is hoped they will be back by September … The king [of England] has
spoken to me several times on the subject. He hopes the affair may turn out
profitable. I believe the distance is not 400 leagues. I told him that I believed
the islands were those found by Your Highnesses, and although I gave him
the main reason, he would not have it.[7]

As we shall see, there was serious trouble brewing with Spain.

The most comprehensive account of Cabot's 1498 voyage comes from the *Great
Chronicle of London*:

This year also the king by means of a Venetian [Cabot] which made
himself very expert and cunning in knowledge of the circuit of the world
and islands of the same, as by a chart and other demonstrations reasonable he
showed, caused the king to man and victual a ship at Bristol to seek for an
island which he said he knew well was rich and replenished with rich
commodities. Which ship thus manned and victualled at the king's cost,
divers merchants of London ventured in [her] small stocks, being in her as
chief patron the said Venetian. And in the company of the said ship sailed
also out of Bristol three or four small ships stocked with small and large
merchandise such as coarse cloth caps, laces, points, and other trifles. And
so departed from Bristol in the beginning of May …[8]

A few weeks after the fleet left Bristol, Pedro de Ayala confirmed Cabot's departure to
King Ferdinand and Queen Isabella, informing them that:

The fleet he prepared, which consisted of five vessels, was provisioned for
a year.[9]

So, we know that he left Bristol in early May with five ships, with himself in com-
mand of the largest vessel. This flagship was provided by the king – Henry made a real
investment in the voyage on this occasion. Interestingly, the other four ships in the
fleet were, according to the *Great Chronicle*, funded by merchants from London,
although the ships might still have come from Bristol. We know more about Cabot's
crew members; in the letter to his brothers in Venice Pasqualigo wrote:

... and [the king] has given him all the prisoners ... that they may go with him, as he [Cabot] has requested.[10]

More significantly, Cabot's crew also included priests – which concerned the Spanish ambassador, Pedro de Ayala, because a priest was part of the process by which a nation laid claim to new territory. Raimondo de Soncino wrote to the Duke of Milan in December 1497:

> I also believe that some poor Italian friars will go on this voyage, who have the promise of bishoprics. As I have made friends with the Admiral, I might have an archbishopric if I chose to go there ...[11]

Cabot's plan was clear: he intended to sail west across the Atlantic and trade with the fabled lands of the Orient. Not surprisingly, the Spanish monarchs felt threatened by what looked like an English incursion into their territory in the New World. According to Raimondo de Soncino:

> But Messer Zoane has his mind set upon even greater things, because he proposes to keep along the coast from the place at which he touched, more and more towards the east, until he reaches an island which he calls Cipango, situated in the equinoctial region, where he believes that all the spices of the world have their origin, as well as the jewels ... and they will go to that country and form a colony. By means of this they hope to make London a more important mart for spices than Alexandria.[12]

Cabot had great hopes for the voyage. Unlike Columbus, who was a deeply religious man with ambitions to convert the local population to Christianity, Cabot's motivations seem to have been entirely secular – he wanted to find a quick and easy route to the Orient so that he could lay the foundations for a thriving mercantile enterprise.

☙☙☙☙☙☙☙

In the end, the 1498 venture appears to have ended in ignominious failure. Soon after departure one of Cabot's ships returned to port after suffering damage in a storm. Pedro de Ayala wrote to the Spanish monarchs:

> News has come in that one of these [Cabot's ships] ... has made land in Ireland in a great storm with the ship badly damaged. The Genoese [Cabot] kept on his way.[13]

Of the remaining four vessels in the fleet nothing more was ever heard. The circumstances surrounding the disappearance of these ships is one of the great unresolved mysteries of maritime history. Their fate has been the subject of much speculation, but there are essentially three possible options: the other ships were lost without trace somewhere in the Atlantic; Cabot returned disgraced and was never heard of again; or at least part of the fleet succeeded in crossing the Atlantic only to perish in some other way. There is, surprisingly, more evidence to support the last theory, but first we should consider the other two.

The simplest explanation is that Cabot's remaining four ships foundered at sea during the crossing. Certainly there was a bad storm that forced one ship back to Ireland. An Italian chronicler of the time made reference to Cabot in around 1512–13, suggesting that he ended up:

> … on the very bottom of the ocean, to which he is thought to have descended together with his boat … since after that voyage he was never seen again anywhere.[14]

Even the great American maritime historian and Columbus expert, the late Admiral Samuel Morison, considered this the most likely outcome. But others disagree. The British historian Dr James Williamson has pointed out that never in the history of trans-Atlantic exploration since 1500 has a multi-ship fleet completely disappeared as the result of an unknown disaster, and he argues that this is unlikely to have happened to Cabot. Pedro de Ayala made it clear that, as far as he knew, Cabot had not perished in the storm with the words *'The Genoese kept on his way'*.

It is worth remembering that by this time Cabot was one of the most experienced mariners of his day. Moreover, this expedition was better funded than the previous year's and it is reasonable to suppose that the ships were well built and well equipped. The possibility that the rest of the fleet foundered during the crossing cannot be altogether discounted, but, as we shall see, there is sufficient secondary evidence to suggest that this is not the way the expedition met its end.

The second possibility is that Cabot returned to England and that his subsequent death went unreported (at least, no record of his death has been found; Cabot was in his late forties – an old man by fifteenth-century standards). His pension continued to be drawn until 1499,[15] and it is thought he may have drawn the monies himself. However, when he left in 1498 his ships were victualled for a year and he was not expected to return until the summer of 1499 at the earliest. His wife Mattea and their three sons were living in Bristol and, in his absence, the pension was almost certainly paid to his family by the Bristol customs, as agreed with the king. Of course, this does not rule out the possibility that Cabot returned in 1499 and continued to collect his pension but died shortly afterwards. So far no historical evidence has come to light to support these possibilities. It is even possible that he returned to England and subsequently decided to go back to his native Italy.

That leaves the third and by far the most intriguing possibility: did John Cabot, with his fleet of four surviving ships, reach North America for a second time? If so, how far did he then travel and why did he not return to England with news of his success?

◎◎◎◎◎◎◎

There is substantial evidence that at least part of Cabot's fleet landed in North America in 1498, and it comes from three quite unrelated sources. First is the evidence from the archives of the Portuguese mariner, Gaspar Corte-Real. During the summer of 1500, Corte-Real crossed the Atlantic and landed at a latitude of about 50°N – probably on the northern peninsula of Newfoundland. After making a brief reconnaissance he returned to Portugal.

The following year Corte-Real mounted a full expedition, this time with three caravels, and returned for a better look. By coincidence, it was Lorenzo Pasqualigo's brother Pietro who reported on the voyage in his capacity as Venetian ambassador to the royal court in Lisbon. Pietro Pasqualigo recounted how Corte-Real found land two thousand miles (3200 kilometres) from Portugal *'between the north and the west'*,[16] that the fleet followed the coastline continuously for six or seven hundred miles (950–1100 kilometres) and that it was assumed they had found the mainland. The fleet returned to Portugal with seven Indians – men, women and children – clothed mainly in otter skins. Pasqualigo reported that these people appeared to have no iron but made knives from stone. He then added a remarkable piece of information:

> And yet these men have brought from there a piece of broken gilt sword
> which certainly seems to have been made in Italy. One of the boys was
> wearing in his ears two silver rings which without doubt seem to have been
> made in Venice, which makes me think it to be mainland, because it is not
> likely that ships would have gone there without their having been heard of.[17]

So who left these Italian trinkets in North America?

It is likely that Corte-Real's expedition landed somewhere in Nova Scotia or, possibly – judging from the reported extent of the coastline and the presence of 'very large rivers'[18] – Quebec. The Indians could only have acquired these European goods from Cabot and his men or, possibly, the crew of a Bristolian fishing vessel.

However, it is unlikely that Bristol fishermen sailed as far as Quebec or Nova Scotia during the 1480s as this would have taken them hundreds of miles west of their fishing grounds off Newfoundland. Nor is it likely that Cabot would have left such trinkets during his first voyage as he went ashore only once and reported no contact with the local population.

So is it possible that these Indians acquired the broken sword and Venetian earrings during Cabot's second visit in 1498? If this is the case, the Indians might have taken them during a skirmish with his crew, possibly even wiping out the expedition and plundering the stores. Yet the Indians showed no hostility towards the Portuguese, so it is unlikely that they had obtained the trinkets by force. These small gifts were exactly the sort of items that Cabot took as barter goods and it is quite possible that the Indians were given them during a friendly encounter with the visitors. So there is certainly circumstantial evidence to suggest that Cabot succeeded in crossing the Atlantic a second time and landed on the coast of North America.

The second piece of evidence that Cabot's fleet landed in North America comes from the Spanish themselves. King Ferdinand and Queen Isabella were kept well informed of Cabot's 1498 voyage by their envoy, Pedro de Ayala. The Spanish monarchs were concerned about incursions by the English into what they claimed, by Papal treaty, was their 'New World'. Also, all was not well with the Spanish exploration of the

THE ROCK AT GRATES COVE

One of the enduring Newfoundland legends about Cabot is that he died there after his ship was wrecked at Grates Cove, at the eastern end of the island, in 1498. The story has its origins in a map drawn by the Spaniard Pedro Reinel in about 1503. In 1955 a British geographer, Arthur Davies, published a paper in the journal *Nature* claiming that the incident could be reconstructed from details on Reinel's map.[19] Cabot's ship is supposed to have sunk close to Grates Cove and Cabot, his son Sancio and some of the crew swam ashore. A rock on the shore at Grates Cove apparently bore the inscription *'Io. Cabotto'* along with others, including *'Sanccius'* and *'Sainmalia';* these were interpreted by Davies as a cry for help from the stranded crew – *'Santa Maria save us'.*

Davies never actually visited Grates Cove and the rock in question disappeared in the 1960s; some say it was taken by archaeologists, others by a film producer who keeps it at his home in the American mid-west! The Grates Cove legend is a fascinating story that is still held dear by people local to the area, but it is given little credence by historians.

West Indies. By 1498 Columbus was on his third voyage across the Atlantic – but still there was no sign of the fabled riches of the Orient despite the Grand Admiral's firmly held belief that he had discovered the islands lying off Cathay. Even when he anchored briefly in August 1498 off the mainland of South America (in the Gulf of Paria in what is now Venezuela), Columbus did not realize that a huge, previously unknown landmass lay to the south. In fact, he almost certainly did not bother to go ashore. Nor was he aware that another vast continent lay over the horizon to the north. By this time the explorer was ill and experiencing mood swings and delusions;

he suffered attacks of blindness, he had gout and he was sleeping badly. His judgement had become increasingly questionable and he could not contain a growing rebellion in the rest of his fleet, which was dispersed among the islands of the West Indies. Columbus was not proving the leader that the Spanish monarchs expected. Strategically, this created a worrying situation for Isabella and Ferdinand at the very time that the English king had sent a fleet of five well-provisioned ships on a mission of exploration across the North Atlantic!

The King and Queen of Spain appear to have sought a solution to the problems of English incursion and Columbus's mismanagement in Alonso de Hojeda, a man who had a well-deserved reputation as a cutthroat and ruthless buccaneer. Hojeda had captained one of the ships on Columbus's second voyage and even then, when still in his early twenties, had acquired a reputation for brutality. He thought nothing, for example, of lopping the ears off local Indians who were suspected of stealing.

While Columbus was on his third voyage Hojeda was given copies of his charts of the New World and dispatched from Spain with three ships in May 1499, exactly a year after Cabot had left Bristol on his final voyage. With Hojeda were two men who were to play significant roles in the story that is about to unfold: one was the Florentine banker, Amerigo Vespucci, who was soon to give his name to the northern and southern continents of the New World; and the other was Juan de la Cosa, an experienced mapmaker who had also sailed with Columbus on a previous voyage to the New World.

Hojeda wasted little time in resuming his old tricks. Unhappy about the condition of one of his ships, he put into Puerto de Santa Maria in Spain and requisitioned a better ship, leaving the old one in exchange. While at sea, he resorted to faking distress so that his men could board passing ships and rob them. And on arrival in the Canary Islands he ransacked the house of the daughter of Doña Beatriz Enríquez de Harana. Not only was Doña Beatriz a woman of high standing in the islands' Spanish community, she was the mistress of no less than Christopher Columbus and the mother of his son Fernando!

By the middle of 1499 Hojeda had made landfall in South America and was working his way west along the coast. His three ships passed through the Gulf of Paria, where Columbus had made his South American landfall almost exactly a year previously; Hojeda continued his brutal regime, fighting, robbing and killing the local population as he went. Then he continued west into previously unexplored territory, past the island of Curaçao into a large gulf which the Indians called Coquibaçoa. Hojeda named the region Venezuela, or 'Little Venice', after a native village that was built out over the water on stilts. He killed more than a dozen Indians, looting their stilt-houses for gold and carrying off a young woman to be his mistress and interpreter.

At this point in Hojeda's exploration of the northern coastline of Venezuela we come across one of the most enigmatic and surprising statements in the whole of the Cabot story. In 1829 the respected Spanish historian Martin Fernández de Navarrete wrote in his authoritative history of the early Spanish voyages of discovery:

> It is certain that Hojeda in his first voyage [i.e. that of 1499] encountered certain Englishmen in the vicinity of Coquibaçoa.[20]

If this is true, it is an astonishing revelation. Not only do we know that everyone returned from Cabot's 1497 voyage, but there is no record of any other English fleet making the voyage across the Atlantic before 1500. We are left with only one explanation: that these *'certain Englishmen'* were members of Cabot's 1498 expedition and – if he had survived – Cabot himself. If this is indeed the case, they must have sailed the full length of the eastern seaboard of North America and crossed the Caribbean from north to south before running into Hojeda and his fleet in Venezuela. An extraordinary achievement by any standards! After a momentous voyage of more than 3000 miles (4800 kilometres) from Newfoundland to Venezuela, Cabot and his crew would have had a better idea than anyone else alive of the sheer scale of the continent whose eastern coastline they had successfully navigated.

It is not absolutely certain why Hojeda was sent out to the New World, but, as we have seen, it is reasonable to assume that the Spanish monarchs were worried that Columbus was losing his grip and that they were also concerned about an English incursion into territory Spain had already claimed. Hojeda had demonstrated his ruthlessness, not only to the native American Indians, but to his own people as well. So Cabot and his crew would almost certainly have met an unfortunate end had they crossed Hojeda's path in Coquibaçoa.

But, like so many elements of the Cabot story, this reference to *'certain Englishmen in the vicinity of Coquibaçoa'* is not without its own uncertainties. Martin Fernández de Navarrete was a historian who was usually assiduous over quoting his sources. On this occasion, though, he was not, so we have no way of knowing what basis he had for making such an assertion. Although the relevant passage starts *'It is certain'*, suggesting that this meticulous scholar was sure of his facts, the lack of supporting evidence is frustrating. Fortunately, there is other evidence in the historical record to support the contention that Cabot's ships may have worked their way south as far as South America, and this corroborating information also comes from Spanish sources.

When Hojeda returned to Spain he was not questioned about his many acts of piracy. Instead, the Spanish monarchs asked him to return to Venezuela to establish a trading post and awarded him the title of Governor of Coquibaçoa. This time his instructions were:

> 'Item: that you go and follow that coast which you have discovered, which runs east and west, as it appears, because it goes towards the region where it has been learned that the English were making discoveries … in order that it be known that you have discovered that land, so that you may stop the exploration of the English in that direction.'[21]

It is clear from other documents of the time that Hojeda was now favoured by the Spanish monarchs. Part of the licence that the sovereigns awarded him contains further reference to what appear to have been encounters with Englishmen in the area:

> 'Likewise their Majesties make you a gift in the island of Hispaniola [now Haiti and the Dominican Republic] of six leagues of land … for the stopping of the English, and the said six leagues of land shall be yours forever.'[22]

Together, the trinkets found by Corte-Real and the Spanish references to Englishmen present a compelling argument. It could be that John Cabot – or at least surviving crew members – successfully explored the eastern seaboard of North America and crossed the Gulf of Mexico during 1498 and 1499. On encountering Hojeda in Coquibaçoa, probably in August 1499, it is likely that they were killed to stop them making a territorial claim on behalf of the English king.

But there is still more evidence. It is found in a remarkable map produced in 1500 by Juan de la Cosa, the cartographer introduced earlier as having accompanied Hojeda on his mission for the Spanish monarchs. De la Cosa had also sailed with Columbus. On both expeditions he travelled through the southern part of the Caribbean and along the northern coast of South America, past what is now Guyana and Venezuela. As an experienced mapmaker, one of de la Cosa's main tasks would have been to survey the region to produce up-to-date charts.

On returning from the voyage with Hojeda he drew up his map, which measures about three feet by six (1 metre by 2 metres) and is now housed in the Naval Museum in Madrid. The map bears the caption *'Juan de la Cosa la fizo en el Puerto de S.Ma. en año de 1500'* – 'Juan de la Cosa made this at Puerto de Santa Maria in the year 1500'. The map was not known before its discovery in a Paris bookshop in 1832, and it has since been verified as authentic. It is particularly significant because it is the very first world map to show the North American continent.

Although de la Cosa surveyed large portions of the Caribbean and the northern coastline of South America, there is no evidence that he (or any other Spanish explorer of the time) sailed north to land on the North American mainland. In fact, the Spanish did not claim to have reached the North American coastline until Ponce de Leon landed on the Florida peninsula in 1513 – thirteen years after de la Cosa produced his remarkable map!

The map shows the Caribbean islands very clearly, including an outline of Cuba. Columbus never succeeded in circumnavigating Cuba and always insisted that the island was a peninsula of the Asian mainland: during one of his more paranoid moments he forced the crew of his second voyage – Juan de la Cosa included – to sign a sworn affidavit to just that effect. So did de la Cosa guess correctly that Cuba was an island, or was he perhaps told as much by the Indians? Or could he have got the information from survey notes taken from Cabot's expedition?

The third and truly remarkable element of Juan de la Cosa's map relates to a series of flags that are clearly marked along the coastline of the North American continent. Five flags can be identified, and alongside each is the inscription *'mar descubierto par inglese'* – 'sea discovered by the English'. Here we have the final piece of evidence that John Cabot's crew may well have been the first Europeans to discover and explore the continent's eastern seaboard between Nova Scotia and Florida. Certainly the Spanish had not surveyed the region because they did not land on the continent until 1513; besides, de la Cosa himself credits the English with the discoveries.

The question then remains: did Juan de la Cosa get the information for his map from surveying notes taken from Englishmen who subsequently died – possibly at the hand of Hojeda in Coquibaçoa – or could it have come from another source?

If there was another English expedition on the western side of the Atlantic before 1500, there is no record of it. But when Cabot went to London to see King Henry VII in August 1497 after his first successful voyage, he showed the assembled throng (including Pedro de Ayala, the ambassador from the Court of Spain) a map and a globe which he used to illustrate his discoveries in Newfoundland. Could de la Cosa simply have taken this information – which was almost certainly passed on to the Spanish monarchs – and added it to his own map?

As with so much in this fascinating but ultimately frustrating story of John Cabot and his voyages of discovery, it is impossible to be absolutely certain. Juan de la Cosa was, without doubt, an experienced and respected cartographer and the map is accepted by historians as genuine. Historians also accept that de la Cosa got his information from Cabot, but they have been unable to establish whether this came from the 1497 voyage, via the Spanish ambassador in London, or whether it was new information from the expedition begun in 1498.

De la Cosa had details of Cabot's 1497 voyage with him in Puerto de Santa Maria when he created the map in 1500. However, the historian James A. Williamson has pointed out that the Venezuelan coastline to the west of Hojeda's Spanish flag is very accurately drawn although it had not at that time been explored by the Spanish. Was this another lucky guess by de la Cosa, or had he somehow acquired survey notes for this area too from a non-Spanish source?

By comparison, de la Cosa's depiction of the North American coastline is impressionistic and could represent all or almost any part of it. The scale is imprecise and he shows its orientation incorrectly. Yet de la Cosa's map is actually a better representation than many others drawn at a later date, particularly when it is considered that global geography and cartography were very much in their infancy in 1500.

Five English flags are shown on the map (these do not necessarily indicate actual landing sites and could simply represent a series of landings). In 1497, Cabot only landed on the mainland once and, although the place names on the map are difficult to read, none bear any resemblance to those named by Cabot during his 1497 voyage, such as Cape Bonavista or *New-Founde-Lande.*

The evidence from the map alone is inconclusive. But, taken with the other evidence described in this chapter – the Venetian earrings and broken sword found with the Native Americans; the written instructions given to Alonso de Hojeda by the Spanish crown, with their clear references to an English presence in the Caribbean when no other English expeditions are known to have been in the region; and Navarrete's tantalizing reference to 'certain Englishmen' in Coquibaçoa – the picture becomes much more compelling. If Juan de la Cosa's map was indeed based on information 'liberated' from Englishmen in Venezuela, then Cabot, or at least some of his crew, must have reached the southern Caribbean after exploring and surveying the whole of the eastern seaboard of the North American continent – a total journey

De la Cosa's remarkable chart of 1500 is the first world map to show
the American continents. On the right of the map is the faint outline of Africa
and Europe, probably drawn to a different scale. On the left is North America, the
Caribbean and the coastline of Venezuela. Historians agree that de la Cosa must have
got information from Cabot's expeditions, but did this come from Cabot's 1497 voyage,
or from 1498? Along the north coast of America are five flags, against each is written
'mar descubierto par inglese' – 'sea discovered by the English'. These flags may indicate several
English landings, rather than an exact number. Cuba is clearly shown as an island,
even though Columbus believed that it was a peninsula of the mainland and insisted
that his crew (de la Cosa included) sign an affidavit to that effect. Columbus was also
convinced that there was a sea passage due west of the Caribbean islands,
which led to the riches of the Orient. Instead of showing this opening, de la Cosa
elected to cover the area of the map (which is present-day Mexico) with a vignette
of St Christopher. Was this a coincidence, or did de la Cosa know the truth
about the landmass, but prudently chose not to challenge Columbus in public?

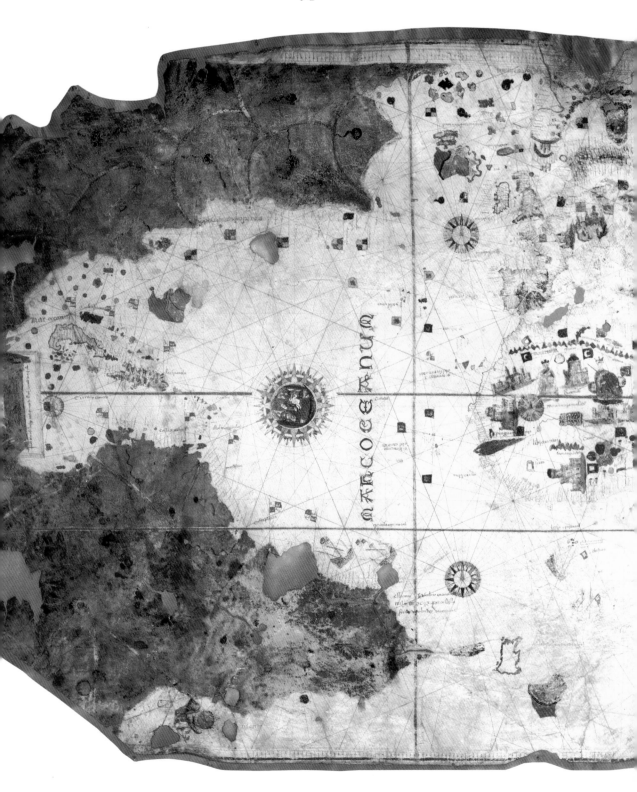

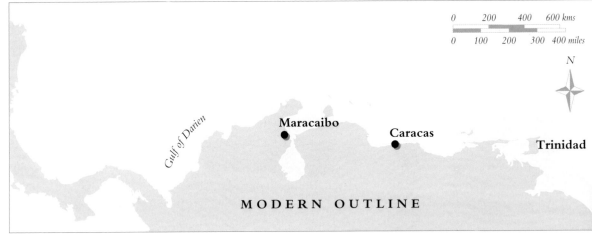

The coastline of Venezuela, comparing the outline of de la Cosa's 1500 map
with that of a modern chart. No part of de la Cosa's map is more accurately drawn
than this section. The eastern part was surveyed by de la Cosa himself when Hojeda's
fleet sailed west from their landfall in Venezuela in the summer of 1499. Hojeda
stopped his westerly passage at Cabo de la Vela. Yet west of this point and even further,
beyond the Gulf of Darien, the map is just as accurate. There is no record of any
Spanish expedition to this region until well after de la Cosa had drawn his map in 1500.
There are no flags or names marked on this mysterious section of coastline.
Did de la Cosa make a lucky guess, or did he get detailed information
from another source?

of more than 5500 miles (8800 kilometres) from their home port of Bristol. To them
should be given the credit not only for one of the most remarkable voyages in
the history of exploration, but also as the true fifteenth-century 'discoverers' of the
continent of North America.

@@@@@@@@

As a postscript, it is worth adding something about the sensitive political situation in 1500. In 1493, Pope Alexander VI divided the spoils of the New World between Spain and Portugal. By the Treaty of Tordesillas, Portugal could claim everything east of a line drawn north–south through the Atlantic 370 leagues west of the Cape Verde Islands (approximately 40°w on today's maps) and Spain everything to the west. This gave Spain rights to most of the Americas, while Portugal could claim Africa. At the end of the fifteenth century Spain and Portugal had dominated maritime exploration for fifty years; England was the usurper and the two other major European players – the French and the Dutch – had barely started. In an attempt to create a political alliance between England and Spain against the French, Ferdinand and Isabella had been in protracted negotiations to marry off their daughter, Catherine, to Henry VII's eldest son and heir, Arthur. These negotiations reached their peak in late 1500 and early 1501. Nothing could be allowed to upset the process, let alone the news that a Spanish agent had wiped out the surviving members of an expedition backed by the King of England.

James A. Williamson has argued that de la Cosa may have deliberately falsified the latitudes shown on his map to give the impression that the English had come much farther south than they actually did and that they were therefore trespassing in Spanish territory. This, he suggested, may have been necessary to provide justification for their murder. When Henry VII issued Cabot with his first letters patent, he chose his words carefully: he said that Cabot could look to the north, east and west but not to the south. On de la Cosa's map the area attributed to the English runs almost due east–west and is on the same latitude as southern England; this was land they were entitled to explore by royal decree. But the area where they may have ended up, in northern Venezuela, was clearly far to the south of any region they had permission to explore! Williamson believes that de la Cosa was a mapmaker of such repute that the error could not have been accidental: the parts reached by the English expedition were intentionally distorted in case news of the murders reached the English king and threw the delicate negotiations over the royal marriage into jeopardy.

In the end, nothing leaked and Catherine married Arthur in November 1501. Arthur died the following year and Henry VII sought papal dispensation for his younger son Henry – who was only twelve at the time – to marry his brother's widow. When Henry VII died in 1509 his son took the English crown as the infamous Henry VIII, and Catherine became his first wife. She bore him six children, only one of whom survived (to become Queen Mary I). Henry's disappointment at not fathering a son led him to divorce her so that he could marry Anne Boleyn; in doing so, he repudiated the Church of Rome. But that, as they say, is another story.

◎◎◎◎◎◎◎◎

Su primera letra es flores

Como quien sal calustar

Como que[...]

Veso mesmo aca en castilla

CHAPTER 8

THE END OF
THE BEGINNING

When 'Grand old men' persist in folly
In slaughtering men and chopping trees,
What art can soothe the melancholy
Of those whom futile 'statesmen' teaze?

EDWARD LEAR *When 'Grand Old Men' Persist in Folly*

The last decade of the fifteenth century was one of the great turning-points in global history, and its consequences were to change the world forever. Several events combined to bring about this dawn of the great Age of Exploration. The medieval period was coming to a close, and the Renaissance – the 're-birth' of classical thought – was already under way, bringing with it a more open and inquisitive society. The fall of Constantinople in 1453 blocked the old trading routes to the Orient and forced European merchants to look west across the Atlantic and south around Africa for new routes to Asia.

Before this time the world was land-centred and primarily inward-looking: contact by sea between different peoples and cultures was relatively insignificant. Europe emerged as if from a chrysalis from the intellectual gloom of the Middle Ages, although her power and importance were still relatively limited. The continent was on the western edge of what was regarded as the civilized world and Europeans looked across the unbroached Atlantic – the 'Sea of Darkness' – into the unknown.

King Ferdinand II of Aragon and Queen Isabella I of Castile, from the Devotionary of Queen Juana the Mad, *c.*1482, painted when they were both in their early twenties. They married in 1469 and united their kingdoms to create the foundations of modern Spain. It was an unlikely match: Ferdinand was described as foxy, deceitful and untrustworthy, and Isabella as precocious, ambitious and far from beautiful.

To the east lay older civilizations; the Ottoman and Safavid empires of the Middle East were still growing and Islam – the most expansive of the world's religions – was making converts in Asia and sub-Saharan Africa. Farther still to the east the Ming Dynasty presided over the greatest and most advanced civilization of the age, for in terms of wealth and population China was far ahead of Europe. This single nation of over 120 million people – larger than the whole of Europe at the time – arguably reached the peak of its artistic and technological achievements during this period.

In the Americas, societies were also sophisticated. Tenochtitlán, the capital of the Aztec empire, had as many as 200,000 inhabitants – nearly twice that of Naples, Milan or Venice, which were the biggest cities in Europe at the time. The Inca empire stretched for 2000 miles (3500 kilometres) along the Andes – the distance from the most northerly cape in Norway to the Mediterranean coast of France. The Incas had a sophisticated road network with over 25,000 miles (40,000 kilometres) of connecting routes, and suspension bridges which crossed chasms up to 230 feet (70 metres) long. They had relay runners who delivered messages up to 150 miles (240 kilometres) a day. By contrast, overland travel in Europe was slow and dangerous; it took an average of nine days to travel the 200 miles (320 kilometres) between Venice and Naples – little better than 20 miles a day.

Despite the relative advancement of other civilizations, the 1490s were to bring changes on a global scale as Europeans took their first tentative steps on a previously unknown continent. By 1522, Magellan's fleet had succeeded in sailing around the world (although Magellan himself did not survive the voyage). Just thirty years separates Columbus's first voyage across the Atlantic from this first full circumnavigation of the globe. Europeans became more outward-looking as they made contact across oceans. The balance of power between the old land-centred civilizations began to change and Europe began to assume the position of overwhelming dominance it was to hold for the next four centuries.

❦❦❦❦❦❦❦

The pioneers of this golden age were the Portuguese. Their close association with the Moors of North Africa allowed them to develop new technology that made the search for new routes possible. The key to long-distance voyaging was the caravel with its lateen sails derived from the Arab dhow. In its day this weatherly vessel represented a revolution almost as significant as the invention of the steam engine or powered flight. These versatile little ships not only crossed oceans, but their shallow draft allowed them to explore safely in uncharted waters close to shore, making the exploration of the African coastline possible.

It was Henry the Navigator who realized the true potential of the caravel. Henry was obsessed with the idea of sailing beyond the known world, and he established what amounted to the world's first naval academy at Sagres, situated on the magnificent headland of Cape St Vincent on the Portuguese Atlantic coast. It was in Sagres that Henry brought together astronomers, cartographers and experienced navigators with all the books, survey notes and charts that he could lay hands on. His tough little caravels and the collective knowledge of his experts allowed the early Portuguese sailors to sail farther and farther down the coast of Africa and return home safely against wind and current. This was the space race of the fifteenth century as Henry's sailors made long, audacious stands out into the Atlantic, into uncharted seas which many still believed poured their waters over the edge of the world in a thundering torrent.

Henry died in 1460 when his pioneers had penetrated only as far as West Africa, but his dream was realized within a generation. What a revelation it must have been when, in 1471, the first sailors crossed the Equator and realized that the ocean did *not* boil as predicted and that humans could (and did) survive quite happily in these tropical regions! By 1486 Bartholomew Diaz had rounded the Cape of Good Hope, and in 1498 Vasco da Gama reached their ultimate goal when he landed on the west coast of India. These achievements became the great state secrets of the age – just as important as nuclear or military secrets today. Such significance was attached to this intelligence that Portugal refused to make her discoveries public and the death penalty was introduced for revealing information about the voyages. This secrecy was understandable: by the end of the fifteenth century 10,000 slaves and 700 kilograms of gold were being imported into Portugal from Africa every year. The age of slavery and of European colonization had begun.

However, such was the blinkered focus of Portugal on her maritime expansion in Africa that the country became isolated from the main political events that were unfolding in the region. The Iberian peninsula was fragmented into a handful of independent kingdoms: along with Portugal, there were the large kingdoms of Castile and Aragon, the smaller states of León, Valencia and Catalonia, and Granada, which was still held by the Moors. Through union and conquest the two big fish swallowed the rest. When Ferdinand, the eighteen-year-old heir to the throne of Aragon, married nineteen-year-old Isabella, sister to Castile's King Henry IV, the stage was set for union. Ten years later, when Ferdinand's father died, Castile and Aragon were united and the foundations of the modern state of Spain were laid through a series of startling reforms and innovations. Isabella and Ferdinand were able to raise their new nation to a position of power and glory that they could never have achieved individually.

Their marriage could not be described as a love-match: Ferdinand was foxy, deceitful and untrustworthy; Isabella was precocious and ambitious and, it was claimed, far from beautiful. But from the beginning she emerged as the dominant partner, and Ferdinand seemed content for it to be that way. A brief war with Portugal allowed the couple to get the measure of each other before they focused their attention on the Moors, who had occupied parts of the Iberian peninsula for eight centuries. The rest of Europe had pursued its crusades against the Saracens in the Holy Land for three and a half centuries. Spain, isolated behind the natural wall of the Pyrenees, was still fighting her own crusade against the Moors, who had dominated the region with their fast, efficient cavalry and religious zeal.

Immensely capable though Isabella was as a ruling monarch, she was also responsible for one of the great abuses of history. The man who brought the Inquisition to Spain was Isabella's confessor, Tomás de Torquemada. What had started in the thirteenth century as a system for religious conversion had by now become an insidious instrument of state control, and in Spain it became the epitome of evil. The Inquisition turned on the Spanish Jews, who were widely believed to have assisted and supported the Moors. As successful moneylenders, they were universally despised; the fact that they were also great writers and travellers, scientists and physicians, who had contributed more than most to the knowledge and understanding of their age, counted for little. The choice open to Jews was simple: either they renounced their faith and became *conversos* or they were handed over to the Inquisition. The proceedings were secret and appeals were not allowed. Accusers and witnesses remained anonymous. Torture was commonplace. But the ultimate ritual for which the Spanish Inquisition became infamous was the *auto da fé* – a public ceremony that often ended in the death of the victim by burning. In the 18 years that Torquemada was Inquisitor-General more than ten thousand people are believed to have died at the stake, many of them Jews who were found guilty on the flimsiest of evidence.

In January 1492 Granada fell and the Moors were finally driven from the Iberian peninsula by the combined forces of Ferdinand and Isabella. Spain was free and ready to turn her sights westwards. Christopher Columbus had been stalking the corridors of the royal courts of Europe for years in quest of a sponsor. Within weeks of the Moors' expulsion Queen Isabella agreed to support him in his search for the Orient and the seeds of a Spanish empire were sown. Yet the events of the previous two or three decades were to have a significant influence on what was about to happen.

As the Jews fled in their thousands they deprived the country of their energy, industry and culture – and also of their wealth. The monetary crisis that followed was only resolved by the influx of gold and silver from the New World. What Columbus began as a search for a spice route and an opportunity to convert the heathen to

Columbus in Chains, by Lorenzo Delleari (1840-1908). During his third voyage,
Columbus was arrested, shackled in irons and taken back to Spain. He insisted on
wearing his chains until the queen removed them, but the Spanish monarchs refused to
restore him to his former position. Columbus obtained royal support for another voyage
to continue his search for a passage to the Orient, but only four worm-eaten
caravels were put at his disposal.

Christianity became a single-minded and ruthless search for wealth. The individuals
responsible for the ensuing barbaric assault on the unsuspecting natives of the
Americas were the conquistadors – knights and foot soldiers whose fighting skills had
been honed on the Moors. After their successful crusade against Islam, this army of
mercenaries found a brief outlet in the war with Italy. But they were soon to turn
their eyes – still fired with religious zeal – towards the west, where there were new
infidels to fight. The Spanish invasion of the Americas was not only the first step in
the growth of modern colonial empires, it was also the last of the great medieval
crusades. It is ironic that these very men, who must all have witnessed the horror of
the *auto da fé*, should profess such outrage in the Americas when confronted with
human sacrifice in the name of another religion.

Once Columbus had secured the support of Queen Isabella he was appointed admiral, viceroy and governor-general of all the islands and mainland that he might discover in the western ocean; he was also entitled to one-tenth of all the profits from the voyage! Yet Columbus had a cranky reputation among Spanish merchants and sailors and he got short shrift in the main ports of Seville and Cadiz. He eventually found backing in the tiny sea port of Palos de la Frontera, but only because the town was obliged to provide two caravels as a punishment for acts that were detrimental to the crown. His tiny inadequate fleet consisted of an eighty-ton carrack called the *Santa Maria* and two small caravels, the *Pinta* and the *Niña*. Columbus sailed in August 1492 with about a hundred sailors and adventurers. During the crossing members of the crew plotted to pitch him overboard while abstracted in his machinations with new-fangled and unwieldy navigational instruments. But, on 12 October – just as the mutinous feelings were reaching a peak – land was sighted.

By March 1493 Columbus was back in Spain with evidence of his discoveries – an exotic cavalcade of six native islanders, crude gold ornaments, plants, animals and birds. It was enough to ensure his place in history – and a new fleet of ships. When Columbus set off on his second voyage he sailed with three carracks, seventeen caravels and fifteen hundred men, an expedition that was remarkably well equipped for the times.

Columbus himself was a complicated man: he claimed to hear celestial voices and he embarrassed the Spanish monarchs by appearing provocatively attired in public – once in chains and frequently in the habit of a Franciscan friar. He was socially ambitious and at times obsessively pig-headed, yet he was awkward in public and frequently struck by self-doubt. He was a mystic, a committed Christian, an opportunist and a fanatical navigator. For a few short years he was one of the most celebrated men in Europe. Yet the crew of this second voyage carried with them the seeds of his eventual downfall, and it was on this next expedition that the contradictions of the Spanish conquest of the New World became apparent. Apart from the usual mix of sailors, artisans and priests, many of the crew were miners – which gives a clue to the aspirations of the expedition's backers. However, most were soldiers of fortune whose main interest was personal glory and profit.

Although Columbus sailed a third and fourth time to search for a western passage to Asia, he fell from favour with the royal court. He returned to Spain for the last time in November 1504, still convinced that he had found Cathay but frustrated by his inability to find the elusive passage that would take him to the fabled riches. He was never to sail again. The final months of his life were marked by illness and vain attempts to secure a restitution of his privileges from King Ferdinand. He died a broken man on 20 May 1506 at Valladolid. Spanish interests in the New World, like those of Columbus, were divided between greed and a religious mission to convert the heathen. As the wretched Carib Indians were to discover, this conflict of interests was irreconcilable.

☺☺☺☺☺☺☺

The island of Hispaniola bore the brunt of the first demands — and the first brutality — of the new arrivals. The Spanish were expecting a quick dividend from their investment in the New World and the instant solution was slaves. American Indians taken into slavery never proved as resilient as Africans and, since so many died, the trade was soon found to be unprofitable. So Columbus concentrated on gold, although he did write in his journal:

> … as many slaves as can be sold … in the name of the Holy Trinity … although at present they die on shipment, this will not always be the case …[1]

The search for gold began the reign of terror on Hispaniola. Every three months the Indians were forced to donate a hawk's bell filled with gold dust — the hawk's bell was a small trinket the Spanish used for barter. In return, the Indians received a copper token stamped with the month which they wore around their neck. However, there were no rich goldfields on Hispaniola and it became impossible to meet the constant demand for this precious metal. Once the Indians had parted with what few gold ornaments they possessed they fled into the hills, only to be hunted down with dogs and killed as an example to others. Those found without a current copper token had their hands cut off. On Hispaniola alone it is estimated that between 1494 and 1508 more than three million natives died as a result of violence or forced work on mining and agricultural projects or were sent to Spain as slaves.

The Spanish crown approved enforced labour, known as *encomienda,* in the New World in 1503 and the first sugar-cane mill was established in 1509 — a sign of things to come. As one newcomer announced: *We came here to serve God, and also to get rich'.* The Spanish conquistadors wanted the land and labour of the native Americans; the priests wanted to save souls. Ultimately, both initiatives wrought havoc in the lives of the indigenous peoples. The first robbed them of their freedom and in many cases their lives; the second denied them their culture. Yet, contrary to the stereotype, many sixteenth-century Spaniards agonized over the ethics of the conquest. Important Spanish jurists and humanists argued at length over the legality of depriving native Americans of their land and coercing them into submission to Spanish authority. Henry VII of England, when issuing letters patent, specified that the laws of England must still apply to sailors in the New World and that anyone found raping or defiling

Soon after landing on the island of Hispaniola, the Spanish began their relentless search for gold. Every three months, the Indians were forced to surrender a hawk's bell filled with gold dust. In return they were given a copper token stamped with the date. Those who were found without a current token had their hands amputated as an example to others.

native women was to be punished. However, these ethical debates had little practical effect and the abuses continued.

◎◎◎◎◎◎◎

The New World was no Garden of Eden. On the Caribbean islands and mainland alike tribal warfare was common and, to deter their enemies, some groups practised cannibalism. Legend has it that Carib Indians found the French to be the tastiest and

Spaniards the most indigestible. On the mainland, the Aztecs preyed on other peoples to satisfy their seemingly insatiable demand for human sacrifice. The Aztecs believed that the continuation of human society depended on nourishing the sun and the earth with human blood. It is estimated that 10,000 victims a year – rising to as many as 50,000 on the eve of the Spanish conquest – had their beating hearts ripped from their chests by the Aztec priests as a sacrifice to their gods. Yet, despite the human sacrifice and cannibalism that was rife in the region, the reality of what was about to befall the native American people almost defies belief.

The two most powerful groups at the time were the Aztecs and the Incas. At the turn of the century the Aztec empire was at the peak of its power. More than 12 million people occupied much of present-day Mexico and the Yucatan peninsula – an area larger than the Iberian peninsula – ruled by the undisputed authority of their emperor, Moctezuma I. The capital, Tenochtitlán, was a huge island city on Lake Texcoco that was linked to the mainland by a sophisticated network of causeways. The Aztecs' rise to power was based in part on farming and irrigation skills, but the real power of the empire lay in the imperial army, which waged war without provocation to secure an adequate supply of captives for sacrifice to their principal god, Huitzilopochtli.

This was the nation into which Hernán Cortés and his conquistadors marched in 1519. The conquistadors – children of the Spanish Inquisition and blooded in the crusade against the Moors – saw only the work of Satan in the ritual human sacrifice of its priests. When Cortés laid siege to Tenochtitlán the slaughter was horrific. The historian W. H. Prescott wrote one of the most celebrated accounts of the conquest of the city:

> The besieged, hemmed in, like deer surrounded by the huntsman, were
> brought down on every side. The carnage was horrible. The ground was
> heaped up with slain, until the maddened combatants were obliged to climb
> over the human mounds to get at one another. The miry soil was saturated
> with blood, which ran off like water, and dyed the canals themselves with
> crimson. All was uproar and terrible confusion. The hideous yells of the
> barbarians; the oaths and execrations of the Spaniards; the cries of the wounded;
> the shrieks of women and children; the heavy blows of the Conquerors: the
> death-struggle of their victims; the rapid, reverberating echoes of musketry;
> the hissing of innumerable missiles; the crash and crackling of blazing build-
> ings, crushing hundreds in their ruins; the blinding volumes of dust and
> sulphurous smoke shrouding all in their gloomy canopy,– made a scene
> appalling even to the soldiers of Cortés, steeled as they were by many a rough

passage of war, and by long familiarity with blood and violence … At length, sated with slaughter, the Spanish commander sounded a retreat. It was full time, if, according to his own statement,– we may hope it is an exaggeration,– forty thousand souls had perished![2]

The Spanish killed millions of people and destroyed virtually the entire rich Aztec culture. One of the few Aztec documents to survive the Spanish destruction records this response by Cortés's lieutenant, Pedro de Alvarado, to a ceremonial dance:

They [Alvarado and his soldiers] attacked the man who was drumming and cut off his arms. Then they cut off his head, and it rolled across the floor. They attacked all the celebrants, stabbing them, spearing them, striking them with their swords. They attacked some of them from behind, and these fell instantly to the ground with their entrails hanging out. Others they beheaded … or split their heads to pieces. … They slashed others in the abdomen … Some attempted to run away, but their intestines dragged as they ran … No matter how they tried to save themselves, they could find no escape.[3]

When Hernán Cortés attacked the Aztec capital he was just thirty-six years old. Two years previously he had set out with a score of ships and a handful of men with the intention of establishing a small colony and amassing a modest fortune. In his wildest dreams he could not have imagined he would discover a immense empire, its cities and monuments as imposing as anything in Europe, ruled by an emperor more wealthy, more powerful and more feared than his own. He started as a buccaneer leading a small band of mercenaries; now he was conqueror of a land larger and richer than that of his own king and queen.

The moral dilemma of the victors in Mexico was neither simple nor straightforward. The Spanish had but two choices over the practice of human sacrifice: they could condone it or they could suppress it. Three hundred years later the British authorities in India faced a similar dilemma when confronted with the practices of infanticide and suttee. From the perspective of the Aztecs and the Hindus the new rulers abused their power in suppressing religious practices which they did not – and could not – understand. Yet Cortés and his soldiers saw nothing but barbarity in tearing out human hearts from their living hosts; raised in medieval Christian Europe, they saw only evil. In the words of an Arab proverb: *'A man resembles the time he lives in more closely than he resembles his own father'*.

The religion of the Maya was more moderate than that of the Aztecs, but a similar fate awaited them in 1524 at the hand of Pedro de Alvarado. From 1531, it was the turn of the Incas of Peru, whose destruction was begun by Francisco Pizarro and his small contingent of conquistadors. At the time of the first European contact, the Americas are thought to have been inhabited by over 90 million people; by the time the colonists began keeping records, their numbers had already been drastically reduced by war, famine, forced labour and epidemics of diseases introduced by contact with Europeans. Nor was this the end of the persecution of the American Indian; it continued throughout the nineteenth century with the opening of the North American 'Wild' West – and some would argue that it continues to this day.

@@@@@@@@

Meanwhile, as Spain continued her conquest of central America, King Henry VII of England was keen to maintain his initiative in North America, though without quite the zeal and enthusiasm of the Spanish. The king's determination to continue trans-Atlantic exploration troubled Manuel I, the king of Portugal, who now realized the true potential of global exploration after Vasco da Gama's successful voyage to India in 1498. In September 1499 Manuel sent several ambassadors to England to dissuade Henry VII from mounting further English voyages of discovery. This appears only to have convinced the English king that he was on to a good thing, for he listened to them politely before giving £60 to *'the ambassador of Portugal'*, £50 to *'the doctor of Portugal'* and £5 to *'the secretary of the delegation'*. But he refused to concede that the two Iberian kingdoms had a monopoly on trade in the New World, despite the Papal Bull of 1493 to that effect.

In 1501, when all hope of John Cabot's return had faded, a new consortium approached the king – and their request to make a trans-Atlantic voyage was granted the very same day. The organizers were João Fernandes, Francisco Fernandes and João Gonsalves, described as squires of the Azores; and three Bristol merchants, Thomas Asshehurst, Richard Warde and John Thomas. Letters patent were issued in March 1501 authorizing the partners to annex any lands they found which *'are unknown to all Christians'*.[4] The king commanded that explorers who flew the English flag should punish anyone who *'shall commit and perpetrate theft, homicide or robberies or who shall rape and violate against their will or otherwise any women of the islands or countries aforesaid'*.[5] This concern for the wellbeing of native women was unusual for the period; Henry VII was not a prudish man, but he did have a reputation for being considerate – even protective – towards the women who graced his court.

The voyage of 1501 probably landed on the coast of Labrador and a second voyage left the following year. Exactly which part of the American coastline they reached is not clear, although it is known that they concentrated on finding a northwest passage around the continent to the Far East. One ship seems to have become separated from the others and was probably lost in the ice. The expedition returned to England at the end of the summer and the King granted annuities of £10 each to the surviving leaders.

The expedition of 1502 returned with three Algonquin Indians, causing a sensation in Westminster. The London chronicler Robert Fabyan was astonished by their primitive behaviour and wrote:

> These were clothed in beastes skinnes, and ate rawe fleshe, and spake such speech that no man coulde understand them, and in their demeanor like to bruite beastes, whom the king kept a time after.[6]

Henry was intrigued by his trans-Atlantic visitors and they lived at court for several years. However, by the winter of 1504–05 he had lost interest in the consortium, which was getting nowhere. They had established no commercial outposts and, compared to the success of the Spanish, the English expeditions were unprofitable. After December 1504 Henry VII withdrew his support from the Anglo-Azorean syndicate and pinned his hopes on John Cabot's son Sebastian, who was still a young man in his twenties.

Sebastian was almost certainly born in Venice around 1480, before his father moved his family to Valencia – although he later maintained that he was born in Bristol and also claimed that he sailed with his father to Newfoundland in 1497. This misinformation is typical of Sebastian Cabot, who has always been considered a less than trustworthy individual and had the reputation of frequently being economical with the truth.[7] Sebastian capitalized on his father's name and enjoyed the king's favour, including an annuity of £10 a year, paid (like his father's pension) from the revenues of the Bristol customs.

Despite his royal connections, Sebastian did not secure financial backing for a voyage until 1508 or 1509, when he is thought to have reached the coast of present-day Labrador and cruised northward as far as Hudson Bay. Early accounts of the voyage suggest that it lasted a whole year and that in July:

> he found the sea full of large masses of ice which drifted hither and thither, and the ships were in great danger of colliding with them … And by reason of the said ice he was obliged to turn back …[8]

Cortés and the Siege of Tenochtitlán in 1519. The Spanish attacked the Aztec capital with only a few score of men, and massacred thousands in a single day. The celebrated historian W. H. Prescott wrote: 'The carnage was horrible. The ground was heaped up with slain, until the maddened combatants were obliged to climb over the human mounds to get at one another. The miry soil was saturated with blood, which ran off like water, and dyed the canals themselves with crimson.'

Later writers have argued that Sebastian's men became mutinous when he tried to continue north and forced him to turn back. Little came of these new expeditions, although English fishermen from Bristol almost certainly continued to fish in Newfoundland waters.

On his return to England Sebastian found that Henry VII had died and that the new king had other matters on his mind – Henry VIII showed more interest in producing a son and in fighting the French than he did in Atlantic exploration. But it is interesting to speculate why there should have been so little English activity for the next sixty or seventy years. Instead of finding the spices and gold of the Orient, the early English explorers came back with tales of a continent populated by primitive tribes and a barren coastline fringed with pine trees with little commercial potential apart from cod. There may simply have been too little to stimulate further ventures: no luxuries, no treasure – and certainly no route to the Orient.

And so the first period of English maritime discovery drew to a rather inglorious close. The French mounted voyages – including those of Jacques Cartier, who discovered

SAILORS' DISEASES

The voyages of exploration brought new illnesses and diseases to sailors, who already suffered from a variety of ailments. On long ocean voyages there was the risk of scurvy – caused by a deficiency of vitamin C. The Englishman J. Franklin Jameson wrote:

Some did lose all their strength, and could not stand on their feete, then did their legges swel, their sinnowes shrinke as blacke as any cole. Others also had all their skins spotted with spots of blood of a purple colour: then did it ascend up to their ankels, knees, thighes, shoulders, armes and necke: their mouth became stincking, their gummes so rotten, that all the flesh did fall off, even to the rootes of the teeth, which did also almost all fall out.

Sailors returning from the Americas brought with them syphilis, which was unknown in Europe. The first carriers were sailors from the first of Columbus's voyages who returned in 1493, and within five years the disease was endemic to the whole of Europe! The sailors passed the disease on to Neapolitan women during the war of 1494–95, and the women in turn infected mercenary soldiers who had joined the fight from other parts of the continent. On returning home the soldiers took with them the sexually transmitted disease; even far-flung Scotland fell victim by 1497. The symptoms were unpleasant: ulceration of the skin was so severe in some cases that victims wore face masks; eyes and bones became inflamed, and finally the heart and nervous system suffered such damage that a merciful death followed.

Sailors took to the New World a wide range of common European infections, such as typhus, tuberculosis, diphtheria, measles and smallpox. These illnesses were previously unknown in the Americas and had a devastating effect on the indigenous Indians, who had no natural immunity. Millions died from the infections.

the St Lawrence River in 1534 and paved the way for the French colonization of eastern Canada. The Portuguese and Spanish laid claim to vast areas of the newly discovered world and, in the East, opened trading posts as far afield as India, the Philippines and China. Meanwhile, the merchants of Bristol became bitterly disappointed by the failure of their country to establish trading links beyond the confines of Europe. It was not until the time of Henry VII's granddaughter Elizabeth I, who was crowned in 1558, that the main period of English maritime expansion really began, and only after the defeat of the Spanish Armada in 1588 was England's status as a major maritime power confirmed.

◎◎◎◎◎◎◎

Meanwhile, what became of the major players in this drama of exploration?

With the death of Henry VII, Sebastian Cabot switched his allegiance to the Spanish crown. In 1525 he led an expedition to Brazil to the river he named Río de la Plata (Silver River). Cabot had reports that the region contained vast amounts of gold and silver, so, ignoring his orders – which were to explore the east coast of South America and continue on into the Pacific – he began a fruitless search of the area. When he returned to Spain in 1530 he was arrested, found guilty of mismanagement and banished to Africa. He was later pardoned and eventually returned to England. In 1551 he founded the Muscovy Company of Merchant Adventurers, an English trading organization. On his initiative the company financed expeditions in search of the Northwest Passage, which culminated in a series of disasters. Although Sebastian Cabot did not succeed in discovering a passage, he did open up trade between Russia and England.

Christopher Columbus and Sebastian Cabot both died disillusioned men, but at least they passed away in their own beds from natural causes. Others were not quite so fortunate. In 1509 Alonso de Hojeda was sent by the Spanish crown to establish a settlement in the Gulf of Darien (see map on page 144). Hojeda sailed with over a thousand men, including the famous mapmaker Juan de la Cosa. The expedition was a disaster. Hojeda had barely landed when he was attacked by Indians armed with poisoned arrows; he lost seventy men, including the great de la Cosa himself, whose body was reported to have been found *'tied to a tree, looking like a hedgehog bristling with arrows, swollen and mis-shapen, of frightful ugliness because of the poisonous herb'.*[9] It was a tragic end to one of the great cartographers of the age. Hojeda pressed on, having himself sustained serious wounds. His men dropped like flies on the forced march through 400 miles (650 kilometres) of swamp, sometimes chest-deep in mud. The journey took thirty days and Hojeda returned to Jamaica with just twenty men, only to perish from his wounds in a hospital in Santo Domingo shortly afterwards.

Sebastian Cabot, the infamous middle son of John Cabot. Sebastian claimed much
of the credit for his father's voyages and his distortion of history – some would say
his shameless lies – led to decades of misunderstanding of John Cabot's achievements.
Sebastian was born in Venice shortly before 1484, although when it suited him he
claimed that he was born in Bristol. He also maintained that he sailed with his father
to North America in 1497, but there is no independent evidence for this.

162

Hojeda, the man responsible for so much carnage in the New World and who was richly rewarded by the Spanish crown for his efforts, died a pauper without even the money in his purse to pay for a Christian burial.

In old age, crippled from his wounds, Hernán Cortés returned to Spain – where he proved a persistent and quarrelsome thorn in the side of the new Emperor. The age of the *conquistador* was coming to a close and Cortés became an embarrassment to the new monarch. He followed Charles V about, pestered his secretaries with complaints, petitioned for a pension of monumental proportions and was generally a court bore. He wanted to die in Mexico and began his final journey across Spain, intending to sail from Villa Rica. With his health failing, he passed away *en route* in the village of Castilleja de la Cuesta, near Seville, at the age of 63. He died rich in land but short of cash, his personal wealth frittered away on litigation.

Cortés's lieutenant, Pedro de Alvarado, was responsible for the defeat of the Mayans. During the retreat from a reckless charge against the Chichimecs, Alvarado was thrown by his horse and pinned beneath it. He died from his injuries eleven days later. Francisco Pizarro, the subduer of the Incas, died at the hands of assassins with the point of a rapier thrust through his throat:

> … and when he was fallen to the ground, and his wind failing him, he
> cried unto God for mercy, and when he had so done, he made a cross on the
> ground and kissed it, and then incontinent yielded up the ghost.[10]

Pizarro's last moments on earth read like an epitaph to a generation. For sailors and explorers alike, the first decades of the sixteenth century were an age of extraordinary adventure, risk and hardship – much of which ended in violent or unpleasant death. For the major European nations it was an age of struggle and a time for acquiring new lands and taking control of overseas territories. For European merchants, it was a time of great reward; the monopoly of Venice was broken and the Muslim domination of the spice trade brought to a close.

The losers, inevitably, were the native Americans, who lost their land, their culture, and in many cases their lives. All this for the sake of a trade route to the East that never really existed in the first place.

JOHN CABOT – A CHRONOLOGY

In referring to the chronology it should be noted that the medieval year began on 25 March.

c.1450   John Cabot born in Italy, probably in Genoa but possibly Gaëta; son of Egidius (possibly Guilo) Caboto.

1451   Christopher Columbus born in Genoa, the son of a wool-weaver.

1460   Henry the Navigator dies

c.1461   Cabot moves to Venice as a young boy.

1475   English fishing rights off Iceland challenged by Hanseatic League. Bristol fishing badly hit.

1476   Cabot becomes a full citizen of Venice after 15 years' residence.

c.1480   Marries Mattea, a Venetian woman.

1481   Two ships, the *Trinity* and the *George,* sail from Bristol in search of the 'Isle of Brasile'.

1482–84   Cabot buys and sells property in Venice, including houses, meadowlands and saltworks.

1484   A dispute over a marriage settlement as Cabot borrows from his wife. Documents suggest they already have at least two sons, Ludovico and Sebastian, and a third son, Sancio, might also have been born.

1485   Battle of Bosworth. Henry defeats Richard III and is crowned Henry VII of England.

1485–90   Cabot travels to the eastern Mediterranean as an agent for a Venetian mercantile firm and visits Mecca. Becomes convinced that the shortest route to the Orient is west across the Atlantic.

1486   *Summer* Henry VII visits Bristol and notices that the women are suspiciously well dressed despite a decline in trade with Iceland.

c.1489   Bartholomew Columbus, brother of Christopher, tries to persuade Henry VII to back a voyage of exploration across the Atlantic; Henry prevaricates.

1490   Henry VII pays another visit to Bristol and taxes the city and idividuals because of their conspicuous wealth.

The Cabot family move to Valencia, where Cabot becomes a technical adviser to the government on the construction of a new harbour. Spanish documents confirm he now has three sons.

1492   *January* Granada falls to the Spanish.

        April Letters of agreement are drawn up authorizing Columbus to sail with the support of the Spanish monarchs.
August Columbus leaves Palos in southwest Spain on his first voyage.
September Cabot discusses harbour project in Valencia with King Ferdinand.
October Columbus makes first landfall in the Caribbean.

1493   *March* Columbus returns to Spain; Cabot's plan for a harbour in Valencia fails.
April Columbus passes through Valencia on his way to Barcelona to inform Ferdinand and Isabella of his success. Cabot travels to Seville and Lisbon to petition the Spanish and Portuguese kings to finance a trans-Atlantic voyage.
September Columbus leaves on his second voyage with 17 ships and around 1500 men.

c.1494   Cabot leaves Spain for England and settles in Bristol.

1494   *June* Spain and Portugal sign the Treaty of Tordesillas, dividing the discoveries in the New World between the two Iberian states.

1495   The first confirmation that Cabot is living in Bristol.

1496   *March* Henry VII grants Cabot letters patent to sail across the Atlantic in search of new lands.

        Summer Cabot sails from Bristol with one ship but is forced to turn back because of a shortage of food, bad weather and disputes with the crew.
August Henry VII visits Bristol again.

1497   *May* Cabot sails from Bristol in the *Matthew*.
June Cabot lands in North America, probably in northern Newfoundland, southern Labrador or Cape Breton Island. He takes possession of the land for the English king.
July Vasco da Gama sails from Lisbon intending to sail around the Cape of Good Hope to India.
August Cabot sails back to Bristol in just 15 days and travels to London to see Henry VII.
December Henry VII grants Cabot an annual pension of £20.
December/March John Day writes to Columbus (see Appendix 2.6) informing him of Cabot's voyage and future plans.

1498   *May* Cabot mounts a third expedition of four or five ships and 200-300 men. Soon after leaving, one ship is damaged and returns to Ireland. The others continue and are not seen again.

        August Columbus, on his third voyage, sights the mainland of Venezuela; by now he is seriously ill.

1499   *May* Alonso de Hojeda and Juan de la Cosa sail from Cadiz and land in 'little Venice' (Venezuela).
August Mostly likely latest date of John Cabot's death if he succeeded in reaching Venezuela; the exact date and whereabouts are unknown.
September Cabot's pension is paid for the last time.

1500   *May* Gaspar Corte-Real sails for the Americas and discovers land at approximately 50°N, which he names Terra Verde.

De la Cosa produces *mappa mundi* showing the continent of North America and a 'sea discovered by the English'.

1501   *March* Henry VII grants letters patent to the Anglo-Azorean consortium, who sail from Bristol.

May Corte-Real sails again for the Americas and encounters friendly natives in Nova Scotia who have a broken sword hilt and Venetian silver earrings.

June Hojeda is awarded a licence by the Spanish monarchs 'for the stopping of the English'.

November Catherine, daughter of King Ferdinand and Queen Isabella, marries Prince Arthur, eldest son of Henry VII.

1502   Prince Arthur dies and Henry VII seeks papal dispensation to enable his younger son Henry to marry Arthur's widow.

Columbus leaves on his fourth and final voyage in defiance of royal orders. He returns disgraced in 1504.

1504   *November* Queen Isabella I of Castile dies.

1505   *April* Henry VII grants pension to Sebastian Cabot.

1506   *May* Christopher Columbus dies in Valladolid.

1508-09   Sebastian Cabot makes a disastrous trans-Atlantic voyage; he probably reached Labrador and sailed north as far as Hudson Bay. Ocampo completes the first circumnavigation of Cuba, confirming that it is an island.

1509   *April* Henry VII dies; Henry VIII becomes King of England.

1510   *February* de la Cosa killed in Venezuela by poisoned arrows.

April Hojeda dies from his wounds in Santo Domingo, Hispaniola.

1513   Ponce de León makes the first Spanish landing in North America, in Florida.

1516   *January* King Ferdinand II of Aragon dies.

1519-22   Magellan sails to the Spice Islands via the southern tip of South America. Hernán Cortés conquers the Aztecs.

1525   Sebastian Cabot leads a Spanish expedition to the Río de la Plata in Brazil and begins fruitless search for silver. When he returns to Spain in 1530 he is arrested and banished to Africa.

1537   Pope Paul III decrees that native American 'Indians' should be considered human.

1541   *June* Francisco Pizarro, who subdued the Incas, is killed by assassins. Cortés's lieutenant, Pedro de Alvarado, is thrown from his horse and dies of his injuries.

1547   *December* Cortés dies in the village of Castilleja de la Cuesta in Spain.

1557   Sebastian Cabot, now over 80, dies of old age in London.

CONTEMPORARY DOCUMENTS

2.1 Petition of John Cabot and his sons, 5 March 1496

Public Record Office, Chancery Warrants for Privy Seal, ser. II, 146. Text given by Biggar (1911), p.6, and Williamson (1962), pp.203-204.

Memorandum that on the fifth day of March, in the eleventh year of King Henry the Seventh, the following bill was considered by the Lord Chancellor of England at Westminster:

'To the kyng our sovereigne lord:
Please it your highness to your moste noble and haboundant grace to graunt unto John Cabotto, Citezen of Venice, Lewes, Sebastyan and Soncio, his sonnys, your gracious letters patentes under your grete seale in due forme to be made according to the tenour hereafter ensuying. And they shall during their lyves pray to God for the prosperous continuance of your moste noble and royall astate long to enduer.'

2.2 First letters patent granted to John Cabot and his sons, 5 March 1496

Public Record Office, Treaty Roll 178, membr. 8. Latin text first printed by Hakluyt in 1582; reprinted, with English translation given here, by Biggar (1911), pp.7-10, and by Williamson (1962), pp.204-205.

'For John Cabot and his Sons
The King, to all to whom, etc. Greeting: Be it known and made manifest that we have given and granted as by these presents we give and grant, for us and our heirs, to our well-beloved John Cabot, citizen of Venice, and to Lewis, Sebastian and Sancio, sons of the said John, and to the heirs and deputies of them, and of any one of them, full and free authority, faculty and power to sail to all parts, regions and coasts of the eastern, western and northern sea, under our banners, flags and ensigns, with five

ships or vessels of whatsoever burden and quality they may be, and with so many and with such mariners and men as they may wish to take with them in the said ships, at their own proper costs and charges, to find, discover and investigate whatsoever islands, countries, regions or provinces of heathens and infidels, in whatsoever part of the world placed, which before this time were unknown to all Christians. We have also granted to them and to any of them, and the heirs and deputies of them and any one of them, and have given licence to set up our aforesaid banners and ensigns in any town, city, castle, island or mainland whatsoever, newly found by them. And that the before-mentioned John and his sons or their heirs and deputies may conquer, occupy and possess whatsoever such towns, castles, cities and islands by them thus discovered that they may be able to conquer, occupy and possess, as our vassals and governors, lieutenants and deputies therein, acquiring for us the dominion, title and jurisdiction of the same towns, castles, cities, islands and mainlands so discovered; in such a way nevertheless that of all the fruits, profits, emoluments, commodities, gains and revenues accruing from this voyage, the said John and sons and their heirs and deputies shall be bounden and under obligation for every their voyage, as often as they shall arrive at our port of Bristol, at which they are bound and holden only to arrive, all necessary charges and expenses incurred by them having been deducted, to pay to us, either in goods or money, the fifth part of the whole capital gained, we giving and granting to them and to their heirs and deputies, that they shall be free and exempt from all payment of customs on all and singular the goods and merchandise that they may bring back with them from those places thus newly discovered.

And further we have given and granted to them and to their heirs and deputies, that all mainlands, islands, towns, cities, castles and other places whatsoever discovered by them, however numerous they may happen to be, may not be frequented or visited by any other subjects of ours whatsoever without the licence of the aforesaid John and his sons and of their deputies, on pain of the loss as well of the ships or vessels daring to sail to these places discovered, as of all goods whatsoever. Willing and strictly commanding all singular our subjects as well by land as by sea, that they shall render good assistance to the aforesaid John and his sons and deputies, and that they shall give them all their favour and help as well in fitting out the ships or vessels as in buying stores and provisions with their money and in providing the other things which they must take with them on the said voyage.

In witness whereof, etc.

Witness ourself at Westminster on the fifth day of March.

By the King himself, etc.'

2.3 Lorenzo Pasqualigo to his brothers in Venice, 23 August 1497

From the MS *Diarii* of Martin Sanuto. Venice, Biblioteca Marciana, MSS Ital. cl. VII, Cod. 417 (vol. I) fol. 374v. Italian text with translations in Biggar (1911), pp.13-15, and in Williamson (1962), pp.207-208

'[London, 23 August 1497] That Venetian of ours who went with a small ship from Bristol to find new islands has come back and says he has discovered mainland 700 leagues away, which is the country of the Grand Khan, and that he coasted it for 300 leagues and landed and did not see any person; but he has brought here to the king certain snares which were spread to take game and a needle for making nets, and he found certain notched [felled] trees so that by this he judges that there are inhabitants. Being in doubt he returned to his ship; and he has been three months on the voyage; and this is certain. And on the way back he saw two islands, but was unwilling to land, in order not to lose time, as he was in want of provisions. The king here is much pleased at this; and he [Cabot] says that the tides are slack and do not run as they do here. The king has promised him for the spring ten armed ships as he [Cabot] desires and has given him all the prisoners to be sent away, that they may go with him, as he has requested; and has given him money that he may have a good time until then, and he is with his Venetian wife and his sons at Bristol. His name in Zuam Talbot [one of several contemporary renditions of Cabot's name] and he is called the Great Admiral and vast honour is paid to him and he goes dressed in silk, and these English run after him like mad, and indeed he can enlist as many of them as he pleases, and a number of our rogues as well. The discoverer of these things planted on the land which he has found a large cross with a banner of England and one of St Mark, as he is a Venetian, so that our flag has been hoisted very far afield.'

2.4 News sent from London to the Duke of Milan, 24 August 1497 (This has been attributed to Raimondo de Soncino, although this is unlikely. Soncino only arrived in England on 23 August and was still in Dover on the following day.)

Milan Archives (Potenze estere: Inghilterra). Translation in A. B. Hinds (ed.), *Calendar of State Papers, Milan*, vol. I, no. 535 (1912), and in Williamson (1962), pp.208-209.

'[24 August 1497] News received from England this morning by letters dated the 24th August ... Also some months ago his Majesty sent out a Venetian, who is a very good mariner, and has good skill in discovering new islands, and he has returned safe, and has found two very large and fertile new islands. He has also discovered the Seven Cities, 400 leagues from England, on the western passage. This next spring his Majesty means to send him with fifteen or twenty ships …'

2.5 Raimondo de Raimondi de Soncino to the Duke of Milan, 18 December 1497

Milan Archives (Potenze Estere: Inghilterra). English translation and important parts of the original Italian in A. B. Hinds (ed.), *Calendar of State Papers, Milan*, vol. 1, no. 552 (London 1912), and in Williamson (1962), pp.209-210.

'[London, 18 December 1497] Perhaps amid the numerous occupations of your Excellency, it may not weary you to hear how his Majesty here has gained a part of Asia, without a stroke of the sword. There is in this Kingdom a man of the people, Messer Zoane Caboto by name, of kindly wit and a most expert mariner. Having observed that the sovereigns first of Portugal and then of Spain had occupied unknown islands, he decided to make a similar acquisition for his Majesty. After obtaining patents that the effective ownership of what he might find should be his, though reserving the rights of the Crown, he committed himself to fortune in a little ship, with eighteen persons. He started from Bristol, a port on the west of this kingdom, passed Ireland, which is still further west, and then bore towards the north, in order to sail to the east, leaving the north on his right hand after some days. After having wandered for some time he at length arrived at the mainland, where he hoisted the royal standard, and took possession for the king here; and after taking certain tokens he returned.

This Messer Zoane, as a foreigner and a poor man, would not have obtained credence, had it not been that his companions, who are practically all English and from Bristol, testified that he spoke the truth. This Messer Zoane has the description of the world in a map, and also in a solid sphere, which he has made, and shows where he has been. In going towards the east he passed far beyond the country of the Tanais. They say that the land is excellent and temperate, and they believe that Brazil wood and silk are native there. They assert that the sea there is swarming with fish, which can be taken not only with the net, but in baskets let down with a stone, so that it sinks in the water. I have heard this Messer Zoane state so much.

These same English, his companions, say that they could bring so many fish that this kingdom would have no further need of Iceland, from which place there comes a very great quantity of the fish called stockfish. But Messer Zoane has his mind set upon even greater things, because he proposes to keep along the coast from the place at which he touched, more and more towards the east, until he reaches an island which he calls Cipango, situated in the equinoctial region, where he believes that all the spices of the world have their origin, as well as the jewels. He says that on previous occasions he has been to Mecca, whither spices are borne by caravans from distant countries. When he asked those who brought them what was the place of origin of these spices, they answered that they did not know, but that other caravans came with this merchandise to their homes from distant countries, and these again said that the goods had been brought to them from other remote regions. He therefore reasons that these things come from places far away from them, and so on from one to the other, always assuming that the earth is round, it follows as a matter of course that the last of all must take them in the north towards the west.

He tells all this in such a way, and makes everything so plain, that I also feel compelled to believe him. What is much more, his Majesty, who is wise and not prodigal, also gives him some credence, because he is giving him a fairly good provision, since his return, so Messer Zoane himself tells me. Before very long they say that his Majesty will equip some ships, and in addition he will give them all the malefactors, and they will go to that country and form a colony. By means of this they hope to make London a more important mart for spices than Alexandria. The leading men in this enterprise are from Bristol, and great seamen, and now they know where to go, say that the voyage will not take more than a fortnight, if they have good fortune after leaving Ireland.

I have also spoken with a Burgundian, one of Messer Zoane's companions, who corroborates everything. He wants to go back, because the Admiral, which is the name they give to Messer Zoane, has given him an island. He has given another to his barber, a Genoese by birth, and both consider themselves counts, while my lord the Admiral esteems himself at least a prince.

I also believe that some poor Italian friars will go on this voyage, who have the promise of bishoprics. As I have made friends with the Admiral, I might have an archbishopric if I chose to go there, but I have reflected that the benefices which your Excellency reserves for me are safer, and I therefore beg that possession may be given me of those which fall vacant in my absence, and the necessary steps taken so that they may not be taken away from me by others, who have the advantage of being on the spot. Meanwhile I stay on in this country, eating ten or twelve courses at each meal, and spending three hours at table twice every day, for the love of your Excellency, to whom I humbly commend myself.

London, the 18th of December, 1497'

2.6 John Day to the Lord Grand Admiral

This letter must have been written after Cabot's royal pension was awarded on 13 December 1497. Since mention is made of another expedition *'next year'*, it must have been written before the end of 1497. The medieval New Year began on 25 March, so it is reasonable to assume that the letter was written between mid-December 1497 and mid-March 1498.

Archivo General de Simancas, estado de Castilla, leg. 2, fol. 6. The Spanish text was published by Vigneras (1956) and the English translation given here is from Vigneras (1957).

'Your Lordship's servant brought me your letter. I have seen its contents and I would be most desirous and most happy to serve you. I do not find the book Inventio Fortunata, and I thought that I [he?] was bringing it with my things, and I am very sorry not [to] find it because I wanted very much to serve you. I am sending the other book of Marco Polo and a copy [map] of the land which has been found. I do not send the map because I am not satisfied with it, for my many occupations forced me to make it in a hurry at the time of my departure; but from the said copy your Lordship will learn what you wish to know, for in it are named the capes of the mainland and the islands, and thus you will see where the land was first sighted, since most of the land was discovered after turning back. Thus your Lordship will know that the cape nearest to Ireland is 1800 miles west of Dursey Head which is in Ireland, and the southernmost part of the Island of the Seven Cities [probably Newfoundland] is west of Bordeaux River, and your Lordship will know that he landed at only one spot of the mainland, near the place where land was first sighted, and they disembarked there with a crucifix and raised banners with the arms of the Holy Father, and those of the King of England, my master; and they found tall trees of the kind masts are made, and other smaller trees, and the country is very rich in grass. In that particular spot, as I told your Lordship, they found a trail that went inland, they saw a site where a fire had been made, they saw manure of animals which they thought to be farm animals, and they saw a stick half a yard long pierced at both ends, carved and painted with brazil, and by such signs they believe the land to be inhabited. Since he was with just a few people, he did not dare advance inland beyond the shooting distance of a cross-bow, and after taking in fresh water he returned to his ship. All along the coast they found many fish like those which in Iceland are dried in the open and sold in England and other countries, and these fish are called in English 'stockfish'; and thus following the shore they saw two forms running on land one after the other, but they could not tell if they were human beings or animals; and it seemed to them that there were fields where they thought might also be villages, and they saw a forest whose foliage looked beautiful. They left England toward the end of May, and must have been on the way 35 days before sighting land; the wind was east-north-east and the sea calm going and coming back, except for one day when he ran into a storm two or three days before finding land; and going so far out, his compass needle failed to point north and marked two rhumbs below. They spent about one month discovering the coast and from the above mentioned cape of the mainland which is nearest to Ireland, they returned to the coast of Europe in fifteen days. They had the wind behind them, and he reached Brittany because the sailors confused him, saying that he was heading too far north. From there he came to Bristol, and he went to see the King to report to him all the above mentioned; and the King granted him a pension of twenty pounds sterling to sustain himself until the time comes when more will be known of this business, since with God's help it is hoped to push through plans for exploring the said land more thoroughly next year with ten or twelve vessels – because in his voyage he had only one ship of fifty 'toneles' and twenty men and food for seven or eight months – and they want to carry out this new project. It is considered certain that the cape of the said land was found and discovered in the past by the men from Bristol who found 'Brasil' as your Lordship well knows. It was called the Island of Brasil, and it is assumed and believed to be the mainland that the men from Bristol found.

Since your Lordship wants information relating to the first voyage, here is what happened: he went with one ship, his crew confused him, he was short of supplies and ran into bad weather, and he decided to turn back.

Magnificent Lord, as to other things pertaining to the case, I would like to serve your Lordship if I were not prevented in doing so by occupations of great importance relating to shipments and deeds for England which must be attended to at once and which keep me from serving you: but rest assured, Magnificent Lord, of my desire and natural intention to serve you, and when I find myself in other circumstances and more at leisure, I will take pains to do so: and when I get news from England about the matters referred to above – for I am sure that everything has to come to my knowledge – I will inform your Lordship of all that would not be prejudicial to the King my master. In payment for some services which I hope to render you, I beg your Lordship to kindly write me about such matters, because the favour you will thus do me will greatly stimulate my memory to serve you in all the things that may come to my knowledge. May God keep prospering your Lordship's magnificent state according to your merits. Whenever your Lordship should find it convenient, please remit the book or order it to be given to Master George.

I kiss your Lordship's hands

JOHAN DAY'

2.7 Grant of pension to John Cabot, 13 December 1497

Public Record Office, London, privy seals, 13 Hen. VII, December. Text given by Biggar (1911), p.16, and by Williamson (1962), p.217.

'Henry, by the grace of God King of England and of ffraunce and lord of Irland, To the most reverend fadre in God John, Cardinal archiebissop of Cantrebury, prymate of all England, and of the apostolique see legate, our chaunceller, greeting: We late you wite that We for certaine considerations us specially moevying have yeven and graunted unto our welbiloved John Calbot of the parties of Venice an annuitie or annuel rent of twenty poundes sterling, to be had and yerely perceyved from the fest of thanunciation of our lady last passed, during our pleasur, of our custumes and sub-sidies commying and growing in our Poort of Bristowe, by thands of our custumers ther for the tyme beying, at Michelmas and Estre by even porcions; Wherefor we wol and charge you that under our grete seal ye do make heruppon our letters patentes in good and effectual forme. Yeven undre our Pryve Seal at our paloys of Westminster the xiiith day of Decembre, The xiiith yere of our Reigne.'

[With memorandum in Latin that this was duly done on January 28 following.]

2.8 Warrant for payment of John Cabot's pension, 22 February 1498

Public Record Office, London, Warrants for Issue, 13 Hen. VII, E. 404, Bundle 82. Text given by Biggar (1911), pp.24-25, and by Williamson (1962), pp.217-218.

'Henry by the grace of God King of England and of ffraunce, and lord of Irland To the Tresourer and Chanbrelains of oure Eschequier greting:
Where as We by oure warrant under oure signet for certain consideracions have yeven and graunted unto John Caboote, xx li. [£20] yerely during oure pleasur to be had and perceyved by the handes of oure Custumers in oure poorte of Bristowe, and as we be enfourmed the said John Caboote is dilaied of his payement bicause the said Custumers have no sufficient matier of discharge for their indempnitie to be yolden at their accomptes before the Barons of oure Eschequier; Wherefore we wol and charge you that ye oure said Treasourer and Chambrelains that now be and hereafter shallbe, that ye, unto suche tyme as ye shall have from us otherwise in commaunde-ment, do to be levied in due fourme ij severall tailles, every of theim conteignying x li. upon the Customers of the revenues in our said poort of Bristowe at two usuell termes of the yere, whereof oon taill to be levied at this tyme conteignying x li. of the

Revenues of oure said poort upon Richard Meryk and Arthure Kemys, late Custumers of the same, And the same taill or tailles in due and sufficient fourme levied ye delyver unto the said John Caboote to be had of oure gift by way of rewarde without prest or eny other charge to be sette upon hym or any of theim for the same. And thies our letters shalbe youre sufficient warrant in that behalf. Yeven undre oure prive seal at oure manour of Chene the xxiith day of ffebruary The xiiith yere of oure Reigne.'

2.9 Payments of John Cabot's pension

(i) *Payment of Cabot's pension by Bristol customs, 25 March 1498*
Public Record Office, Exchequer 122, 20/11 (View of Account, Bristol Customs, Michaelmas–Easter, 13 Hen. vii). Original Latin, with translation, given by Biggar (1911), pp.25-27, and by Williamson (1962), pp.218-219.

[Among other items] '… And £10 paid by them to John Calbot a Venetian, late of the town of Bristol aforesaid, for his annuity of £20 a year granted to him by our said lord the king by his letters patent, to be taken at two terms of the year out of the customs and subsidies arising and growing in the said port of the town of Bristol, to wit, for the term of the Annunciation of the Blessed Virgin Mary [25 March 1497] falling within the time of this view, by a quittance of the said John, shown upon this view and remaining in the possession of the said collectors.'

(ii) *Payment of Cabot's pension by Bristol customs, 1498–99*
Westminster Chapter Archives, Chapter Muniments, 12243 (Roll of Accounts of the Bristol Customers for the years 1496-99). Original Latin, in fascimile, in E. Scott and A. E. Hudd (eds), *The Cabot Roll* (Bristol, 1897).

[Among other items, Michaelmas, 1497–Michaelmas, 1498] 'And in the treasury in one tally in the name of John Cabot, £20.' [Michaelmas, 1498–Michaelmas, 1499] 'And in the treasury in one tally in the name of John Cabot, £20.'

2.10 Polydore Vergil on John Cabot

The *Anglica Historia of Polydore Vergil,* edited with a translation from the original
Latin by Denys Hay, Camden Series, vol. LXXIV (Royal Historical Society, 1950),
pp.116-117. The section given here is not in the printed editions but can be found
in Liber XXIV of a MS copy, made in 1512-13, held in the Vatican Library. The names
'Ioanne Cabot' and 'Ioanne' were inserted later in spaces previously left blank
(editor's footnote, p.116). English translation also in Williamson (1962), pp.224-225.

'There was talk at about this time that some sailors on a voyage had discovered lands
lying in the British ocean, hitherto unknown. This was easily believed because the
Spanish sovereigns in our time had found many unknown islands. Wherefore King
Henry at the request of one John Cabot, a Venetian by birth, and a most skilful
mariner, ordered to be prepared one ship, complete with crew and weapons; this he
handed over to the same John to go and search for those unknown islands. John set
out in this same year and sailed first to Ireland. Then he set sail towards the west. In
the event he is believed to have found the new lands nowhere but on the very
bottom of the ocean, to which he is thought to have descended together with his
boat, the victim himself of the self-same ocean; since after that voyage he was never
seen again anywhere.'

2.11 Second letters patent granted to John Cabot, 3 February 1498

Public Record Office, London, Warrants for Privy Seal, c. 82/173,13 Hen. VII,
February. The PRO also holds a Latin copy (Treaty Roll 179, membr. 1). Text given by
Biggar (1911), pp.22-24, and by Williamson (1962), pp.226-227.

'To the kinge
Pleas it your highnesse. Of your moste noble and habundaunt grace, to graunte to
John Kabotto, Venician, your gracious letters patentes in due fourme to be made
accordyng to the tenour hereafter ensuyng, and he shal contynually praye to God for
the preservacion of your moste noble and roiall astate longe to endure.

H[en]R[icus]Rex
To all men to whom thies presentis shall come, send gretyng: Knowe ye that we of
our grace especiall and for dyvers causis us movyng we have geven and graunten and
by thies presentes geve and graunte to our wel beloved John Kaboto, Venician, sufficiente auctorite and power that he by hym, his deputie or deputies sufficient may

176

take at his pleasure vi [6] englisshe shippes in any porte or ports or other place within this our realme of Englond or obeisaunce, so that and if the said shippes be of the bourdeyn of cc [200] tonnes or under, with their apparaill requisite and necessarie for the saveconduct of the seid shippes, and theym convey and lede to the londe and Iles of late founde by the seid John in oure name and by our cammaundemente, paying for theym and every of theym as and if we shuld in or for our owen cause paye and noon otherwise.

And that the seid John by hym, his deputie or deputies sufficiente maye take and receyve into the seid shippes and every of theym all suche Maisters, Maryners, pages and our subiectes, as of their owen free wille woll goo and passe with hym in the same shippes to the seid londe or Iles withoute any impedymente, lett or pertur-baunce of any of our officers or ministres or subiectes whatsoevir they be by theym to the seid John, his deputie or deputis an allother our seid subiectes or any of theym passing with the seid John in the seid shippes to the seid londe or Iles to be doon or suffer to be doon ar attempted. Yeving in commaundement to all and every our offi-cers, ministres and subiectes seying or heryng thies our letters patentes, without any ferther commaundement by us to theym or any of theym to be geven, to perfourme and socour, the seid John, his deputies and all our seid subiectes so passyng with hym according to the tenour of thies our letters patentes, any statute, acte or ordenaunce to the contrarye made or to be made in any wise notwithstanding.'

2.12 Agostino de Spinula to the Duke of Milan, 20 June 1498

Milan Archives (Potenze estere: Inghilterra). Translation in A. B. Hinds (ed.) *Calendar of State Papers, Milan,* vol. 1 , no. 571 (London, 1912), and in Williamson (1962), pp.227.

'[London, 20 June 1498] … There were three other letters, one for Messer Piero Carmeliano, one for Messer Piero Penech, and one for Messer Giovanni Antonio de Carbonariis. I will keep the last until his return. He left recently with five ships, which his Majesty sent to discover new lands.'

2.13 Pedro de Ayala to the Spanish sovereigns, 25 July 1498

Archivo General de Simancas, Estado Tratados con Inglaterra, leg. 2, fol. 196.
The original was sent to Spain with most of the words in cipher and on receipt was deciphered inaccurately. The document was redeciphered by G. A. Bergenroth

in *Calendar of State Papers, Spain* (1862) and again, more accurately, by Biggar (1911), pp.27-29; also given in Williamson (1962), pp.228-229.

'[London, 25 July 1498] … I think Your Highnesses have already heard how the king of England has equipped a fleet to explore certain islands or mainland which he has been assured certain persons who set out last year from Bristol in search of the same have discovered. I have seen the map made by the discoverer, who is another Genoese like Columbus, who has been in Seville and at Lisbon seeking to obtain persons to aid him in this discovery. For the last seven years the people of Bristol have equipped two, three [and] four caravels to go in search of the island of Brazil and the Seven Cities according to the fancy of this Genoese. The king made up his mind to send thither, because last year sure proof was brought him they had found land. The fleet he prepared, which consisted of five vessels, was provisioned for a year. News has come that one of these, in which sailed another Friar Buil, has made land in Ireland in a great storm with the ship badly damaged. The Genoese kept on his way. Having seen the course they are steering and the length of the voyage, I find that what they have discovered or are in search of is possessed by Your Highnesses because it is at the cape which fell to Your Highnesses by the convention with Portugal. It is hoped they will be back by September. I let [?will let] Your Highnesses know about it. The king has spoken to me several times on the subject. He hopes the affair may turn out profitable. I believe the distance is not 400 leagues. I told him that I believed the islands were those found by Your Highnesses, and although I gave him the main reason, he would not have it. Since I believe Your Highnesses will already have notice of all this and also of the chart or mappermonde which this man has made, I do not send it now, although it is here, and so far as I can see exceedingly false, in order to make believe that these are not part of the said islands …

London, 25 July, 1498'

2.14 Pietro Pasqualigo, Venetian Ambassador in Portugal, to his brothers in Venice, 19 October 1501

Paesi nouamente retrouati (Vicenza, 1507), lib. VI, cap. CXXVII. English translation from Williamson (1962), pp.229-230.

'[Lisbon, 19 October 1501] On the eighth of the present month arrived here one of the two caravels which this most august monarch sent out in the year past under Captain Gaspar Corterat to discover land towards the north; and they report that they have found land two thousand miles from here, between the north and the west, which never before was known to anyone. They examined the coast of the same for perhaps six hundred to seven hundred miles and never found the end, which leads them to think it a mainland. This continues to another land which was discovered last year in the north. The caravels were not able to arrive there on account of the sea being frozen and the great quantity of snow. They are led to this same opinion from the considerable number of very large rivers which they found there, for certainly no island could ever have so many nor such large ones. They say that this country is very populous and the houses of the inhabitants of long strips of wood covered over with the skins of fish. They have brought back here seven natives, men and women and children, and in the other caravel, which is expected from hour to hour are coming fifty others. These resemble gypsies in colour, features, stature and aspect; are clothed in the skins of various animals, but chiefly of otters. In summer they turn the hair outside and in winter the opposite way. And these skins are not sewn together in any way nor tanned, but just as they are taken from the animals; they wear them over their shoulders and arms. And their privy parts are fastened with cords made of very strong sinews of fish, so that they look like wild men. They are very shy and gentle, but well formed in arms and legs and shoulders beyond description. They have their faces marked like those of the Indians, some with six, some with eight, some with less marks. They speak, but are not understood by anyone. Though I believe that they have been spoken to in every possible language. In their land there is no iron, but they make knives out of stones and in like manner the points of their arrows. And yet these men have brought from there a piece of broken gilt sword which certainly seems to have been made in Italy. One of the boys was wearing in his ears two silver rings which without doubt seem to have been made in Venice, which makes me think it to be mainland, because it is not likely that ships would have gone there without their having been heard of. They have great quantity of salmon. herring, cod and similar fish. They have also great store of wood and above all of pines for making masts and yards of ships. On this account his Majesty here intends to draw great advantage from the said land, as well by the wood for ships, of which they are in want, as by the men, who will be excellent for labour and the best slaves that have hitherto been obtained. This has seemed to me worthy to be notified to you, and if anything more is learned by the arrival of the captain's caravel, I shall likewise let you know.'

2.15 Extracts from the patent granted by the Spanish sovereigns to Alonso de Hojeda (Ojeda), 8 June 1501

Archivo General de Simancas, Cédulas, no. 5. Original Spanish given by M. Fernández de Navarrete, *Colección de los viages y descubrimientos,* vol. III (Madrid, 1829), pp.85–88. English translation in Williamson (1962), pp.233–234.

Licence to Ojeda to pursue his discoveries on terms including the following:

'Firstly, that you may not touch in the land of the pearl-gathering, of that part of Paria from the coast of the Frailes and the gulf this side of Margarita, and on the other side as far as Farallon, and all that land which is called Citriana, in which you have no right to touch.

Item: that you go and follow that coast which you have discovered, which runs east and west, as it appears, because it goes towards the region where it has been learned that the English were making discoveries; and that you go setting up marks with the arms of their Majesties, or with other signs that may be known, such as shall seem good to you, in order that it be known that you have discovered that land, so that you may stop the exploration of the English in that direction.

Item: that you the said Alonso de Hojeda, for the service of their Majesties, enter that island and the others that are around it which are called Quiquevacoa in the region of the main land, where the green stones are, of which you have brought a sample, and that you obtain as many as you can, and in like manner see to the other things which you brought as specimens in that voyage.

Item: that you the said Alonso de Hojeda take steps to find out that which you have said you have learned of another gathering place of pearls, provided that it be not within the limits above mentioned, and that in the same way you look for the gold-mines of whose existence you say you have news. ...

And their Majesties, in consideration of what you have spent and the service you have done, and are now bound to do, make you the gift of the governorship of the island of Caquevacoa, which you have discovered, during their pleasure ... Likewise their Majesties make you gift in the island of Hispaniola of six leagues of land with its boundary, in the southern district which is called Maquana, that you may cultivate it and improve it, for what you shall discover on the coast of the main land for the stopping of the English, and the said six leagues of land shall be yours for ever.'

ᦂᦂᦂᦂᦂᦂᦂ

NOTES

CHAPTER 1

1   Pastor, Ludwig von, *History of the Popes, from the Close of the Middle Ages*, 2nd edn. F. I. Antrobus and R. F. Kerr, eds (St Louis, Missouri, 1902–10).

2   The recipe given is a mix of several medieval recipes but is based mainly on Brears *et al.* (1993).

3   From the MS *Diarii* of Marin Sanuto, Venice, Biblioteca Marciana MSS Ital. CL.VII, Cod. 417 (vol. 1), fol. 374v. The translation is from Biggar (1911).

4   Adapted from Hartley (1954), pp.225–227.

5   Barlow, R., *A Brief Summe of Geographie*. E. G. R. Taylor ed., Hakluyt Society, 2nd ser. lxix, 1931, p.47.

6   Openheim, M., 'Maritime history'. In *The Victoria History of the Country of Somerset*, ii (London, 1911), p.245.

CHAPTER 2

1   From dispatch of Pedro de Ayala, junior ambassador at the English court, to the Spanish king and queen, 25 July 1498 (given in translation in Appendix 2.13).

2   Milan Archives (Potenze estere: Inghilterra). English translation in A. B. Hinds, ed., *Calendar of State Papers, Milan*, vol. 1, no. 535 (London, 1912); also in Williamson (1962), pp.208–209.

3   Original documents in the Archivo Regional de Valencia, Archivo del Real, Epistolarum vol. 496. Translation from Williamson (1962).

4   MS *Diarii* of Martin Sanuto, Venice, Biblioteca Marciana MSS Ital. Cl.VII, Cod. 417 (vol. 1), fol. 374v. Translation from Biggar (1911).

CHAPTER 4

1   Greenhill (1976), p.236.

2   Friel (1995), p.54.

CHAPTER 5

1   *Navigatio Sancti Brendani Abbatis,* translated in *The Brendan Voyage* by Tim Severin.

2   *Norse Sagas, Hank's Book* and *The Tale of the Greenlanders* (*Groenlendina thattr*); original manuscripts in the Royal Library, Copenhagen.

3   Skelton, R. A., *et al.*, *The Vinland Map and the Tartar Relation* (Yale, 1965).

4   Carns-Wilson, Eleanora, 'The Iceland Trade'. In Eileen Power and M. M. Postan, eds, *Studies in English Trade in the Fifteenth Century* (Routledge & Kegan Paul, 1951), pp.155–182.

5   Hakluyt, Richard, *Voyages* (Dent, 1907).

6   Harvey, John H., *William Worcestre, Itineraries* (Clarendon, 1969).

7   Treaty Roll C76/164, membr. 10, Public Record Office, Kew, London.

8   As note 6, this chapter.

9   Charge against Croft of 1481 in the Bristol customs records; held at the Public Record Office, Kew, London, as F.122/19, 16. Translation from Williamson (1962), pp.188–189.

10 Storey, R. L., *Henry VII, after John Leland, De Rebus Britannicis Collectanea*, vol. 4. Thomas Hearne, ed. (London, 1774), p.200.

11 Vigneras (1957) pp.219-228.

CHAPTER 6

1   Letters patent granted by Henry VII to John Cabot and his sons; text given in Appendix 2.2.

2   Appendix 2.6.

3   The *Rolls of Oléron* (c. 12th century) are named after an island in the Bay of Biscay and represent the earliest maritime code to appear beyond the Mediterranean. They became the nucleus of maritime law in England, France, Scotland and Castile, among other countries, and are still occasionally cited in modern courts.

4   Hastings MS, 1480.

5   Soncino's letter is dated 18 December 1497; a full transcript is given in Appendix 2.5.

6   Parts of the content of the Fust document were preserved as copied extracts. See Williamson (1962), p.57.

7   Appendix 2.6.

8   Letter dated 23 August 1497; full text given in Appendix 2.3.

9   Appendix 2.6.

10 Letter of 18 December 1497 (Appendix 2.5).

11 Morison (1971), pp.130-131.

12 Letter of Lorenzo Pasqualigo, 23 August 1497 (Appendix 2.3).

13 Letter of John Day (Appendix 2.6).

14 *Ibid.*

15 *Ibid.*

16 *Ibid.*

17 *Ibid.*

18 Morison (1971), pp.130-131.

19 Letters given in, respectively, Appendices 2.6, 2.3 and 2.4.

20 Letter of 18 December 1497 (Appendix 2.5).

21 Appendix 2.6.

22 Letter of 18 December 1497 (Appendix 2.5).

23 Appendix 2.6.

24 *Ibid.*

CHAPTER 7

1   Letter of 18 December 1497 (Appendix 2.5).

2   Letter of 23 August 1497 (Appendix 2.3).

3   *Ibid.*

4   Letter of 24 August 1497 (Appendix 2.4).

5   The pension was granted on 13 December 1497 and confirmed by warrant on 22 February 1498. For the grant, warrant and details of payment see Appendices 2.7-2.9.

6 The letters patent were granted on 3 February 1498; the text of the document is given in Appendix 2.11.

7 Dispatch dated 25 July 1498 (Appendix 2.13).

8 Put into modern English from text in A. H. Thomas and I. D. Thornley (eds), *The Great Chronicle of London* (London, 1939), pp.287-288. Also in Williamson (1962), pp.220-222.

9 Dispatch dated 25 July 1498 (Appendix 2.13).

10 Letter of 23 August 1497 (Appendix 2.3).

11 Letter of 18 December 1497 (Appendix 2.5).

12 *Ibid.*

13 Dispatch dated 25 July 1498 (Appendix 2.13).

14 For this account by Polydore Vergil see Appendix 2.10.

15 The relevant Bristol customs records are given in Appendix 2.9.

16 Pietro Pasqualigo's letter of 19 October 1501 is given in Appendix 2.14.

17 *Ibid.*

18 Pietro Pasqualigo reported that 'They examined the coast … for perhaps six hundred to seven hundred miles and never found the end, which leads them to think it a mainland. … They are led to this same opinion from the considerable number of very large rivers…' (Appendix 2.14).

19 Arthur Davies, 'The last voyage of John Cabot and the rock at Grates Cove.' *Nature, Lond.*, no. 4491, 26 November 1955, pp.996-999.

20 Martin Fernández de Navarrete, *Colección de los viages y descubrimientos*, vol. III (Madrid 1829), p.41.

21 From the patent granted to Hojeda by the Spanish monarchs on 8 June 1501 (Appendix 2.15).

22 *Ibid.*

CHAPTER 8

1 *Cristóbal Colón: Textos y Documentos Completos*, C. Varela, ed. (Madrid, 1984).

2 Prescott (1931).

3 Innes (1986), p.110.

4 Letters patent granted 19 March 1501, held at Public Record Office, Kew, London, as Patent Roll 16 Hen. VII, pt I, membr. 20, 21.

5 *Ibid.*

6 *London Chronicles* on the voyage of 1498. Quoted by A. H. Thomas and I. D. Thornley, *The Great Chronicle of London* (London, 1939), pp.287-288; also given in Williamson (1962), pp.220-222.

7 The historian James A. Williamson (1962, p.97) goes so far as to refer to Sebastian Cabot as 'a shameless liar'!

8 From Peter Martyr's Second Account of Sebastian Cabot's Voyage. *Summario della Generale Istoria dell' Indie Occidentali*, Libro Primo della *Historia dell' Indie Occidentali* (Venice, 1534), f. 65. English translation in Williamson (1962), pp.268-269.

9 Bartolomé de las Casas, *Historia de las Indias*. G. de Reparez, ed. (Madrid, 1929).

10 Innes (1986), p.205.

BIBLIOGRAPHY

Andrews, Kenneth R. *Trade, Plunder and Settlement. Maritime Enterprise and the Genesis of the British Empire 1480–1630* (Cambridge University Press, 1984).

Baddely, St Clair. A Bristol Rental, 1498-9. *Transactions of the Bristol & Gloucestershire Archaeological Society*, Vol. XLVII, 1925, pp. 123-129.

Bass, George F. *A History of Seafaring* (Thames & Hudson, 1972).

Betty, J. H. *Bristol Observed; Visitors' Impressions of the City from Doomsday to The Blitz* (Redcliffe, 1986).

Biggar, Henry Percival *The Precursors of Jacques Cartier, 1447–1534, A Collection of Documents Relating to the Early History of the Dominion of Canada* (Ottawa: Government Printing Bureau, 1911)

Brears, Peter, *et al. A Taste of History* (English Heritage, 1993).

Burwash, Dorothy. *English Merchant Shipping, 1460–1540* (University of Toronto, 1947).

Canby, Urtlandt. *History of Ships and Seafaring* (Prentice-Hall, 1964).

Cohen, J. M. (ed. & trans.). *The Four Voyages of Christopher Columbus* (Penguin, 1969).

Collis, Maurice. *Marco Polo* (Faber & Faber, 1959).

Cook, A. and C. Holland. *The Exploration of Northern Canada 500 to 1920: A Chronology* (The Arctic History Press, 1978).

Cunliffe, Tom. *Topsail and Battleaxe* (David & Charles, 1988).

Darby, H. C. *A New Historical Geography of England before 1600* (Cambridge University Press, 1980).

Davies, Arthur. The last voyage of John Cabot and the rock at Grates Cove. *Nature, Lond.*, vol. 4491, 26 Nov. 1955, pp. 996-999.

Dodd, Jack. *The Wind in the Rigging* (Newfoundland, 1972).

Dodd, Jack. *Cabot's Voyage to Newfoundland* (Newfoundland, 1974).

Dodgshon, R. A. and R. A. Butlin. *An Historical Geography of England and Wales* (Academic Press, 1978).

Dominik, Mark. *Columbus in Canada* (Canada: Beaverton, 1996).

Drummond J. C., and Anne Wilbraham. *The Englishman's Food* (Pimlico, 1991).

Dyson, John. *Columbus – for Gold, God and Glory. In search of the real Christopher Columbus* (Madison Press, 1991).

Fagan, Brian. *Elusive Treasure: The Story of Early Archaeologists in the Americas* (Macdonald and Jane's, 1978).

Fernández-Armesto, Felipe. *Columbus* (Oxford University Press, 1991).

Friel, Ian. *The Good Ship* (British Museum Press, 1995).

Fuson, Robert H. (trans.) *Cristóbal Colón, The log of Christopher Columbus* (Ashford Press, 1987).

Gardiner, Robert (ed.) *Cogs, Caravels and Galleons* (Conway, 1994).

Gilchrist, John H. Cabotian conjectures: Did a Cabot reach Maine in 1498? *American Neptune*, vol. 45 no. 4, 1985, pp. 249–252.

Goldsmith-Carter, George. *Sailors* (Hamlyn, 1966).

Graham-Campbell, James. *The Viking World* (Frances Lincoln, 1980).

Greenhill, Basil. *Archaeology of the Boat* (Black, 1976).

Hartley, Dorothy. *Food in England* (Macdonald and Jane's, 1954).

Huizinga, J. *The Waning of the Middle Ages* (Penguin, 1955).

Ife, B. W. *Christopher Columbus. Journal of the First Voyage (Diario del Primer Viaje)* (Aris & Phillips, 1990).

Innes, Hammond. *The Conquistadors* (Collins, 1986).

Jacob, E. F. (ed.) *The Fifteenth Century 1399–1485* (Oxford University Press, 1969).

Jameson, J. Franklin. (gen. ed.) *The Northmen, Columbus and Cabot 985–1503* (Barnes and Noble, 1906).

Keen, M. H. *England in the Later Middle Ages* (Methuen, 1973).

Kington, J. A. The voyage of the British First Fleet from Portsmouth to Port Jackson in 1787-1788 and its impact on the history of meteorology in Australia. In: *Colonial Observatories and Observations, University of Durham, 8–10 April 1994*, J. M. Kenworthy (ed.), Royal Meteorological Society, Reading, 1996.

Knox-Johnston, Robin. *The Columbus Venture* (BBC Books, 1991).

Koning, Hans. *Columbus: His Enterprise* (Latin American Bureau, 1976).

Labarge, Margaret Wade. *Medieval Travellers* (Camelot, 1982).

Lamb, H. H. *Climate: Present, Past and Future. Vol. 2, Climatic History and the Future* (Methuen, 1977).

Langley, Michael. *When the Pole Star Shone: A History of Exploration* (George Harrap, 1972).

Latham, Ronald (trans.). *The Travels of Marco Polo* (Folio Society, 1958).

Lewis, David. *The Voyaging Stars: Secrets of the Pacific Island Navigators* (Collins, 1978).

Little, Bryan. *John Cabot – The Reality* (Redcliffe Press, 1983).

Litvinoff, Barnet. *1492: The Decline of Medievalism and the Rise of the Modern Age* (Macmillan, 1991).

Manchester, William. *A World Lit Only by Fire. The Medieval Mind and the Renaissance* (Macmillan, 1992).

Morison, Samuel Eliot. *Admiral of the Ocean Sea. A Life of Christopher Columbus* (Little, Brown & Company, 1942).

Morison, Samuel Eliot. *The European Discovery of America: The Northern Voyages, AD500–1600* (Oxford University Press, 1971).

Morris, Roger. *Atlantic Sail: Ten Centuries of Ships of the North Atlantic* (Aurum, 1992).

Parry, J. H. *The Discovery of the Sea* (University of California, 1974).

Polo, Marco. *The Travels of Marco Polo (a modern translation by Teresa Waugh from the Italian by Maria Bellonci)* (Sidgwick & Jackson, 1984).

Prescott, W. H. *History of the Conquest of Mexico* (Random House, 1931). First published in 1843.

Quinn, D. B. The argument for the English discovery of America between 1480 and 1494. *Geographical Journal*, vol. CXXVIII pt 3, 1961, pp. 277-285.

Quinn, D. B. *England and the Discovery of America* (Allen & Unwin, 1974).

Quinn, D. B. Did Bristol sailors discover America? Letter to *The Times*, 30 April 1976.

Quinn, D. B. *Sebastian Cabot and Bristol Exploration* (Bristol Branch of the Historical Association, University of Bristol, 1993).

Ruddock, Alwyn A. John Day of Bristol and the English voyages across the Atlantic before 1497. *Geographical Journal*, vol. 132, 1966, pp. 225-233.

Sale, Kirkpatrick. *The Conquest of Paradise* (Hodder & Stoughton, 1991).

Severin, Tim. *The Brendan Voyage* (Hutchinson, 1978).

Smith, Lesley M. *The Middle Ages (The Making of Britain)* (Macmillan, 1985).

Spectre, Peter H. and David Larkin. *Wooden Ship* (Cassell, 1991).

Tannahill, Reay. *Food in History* (Penguin, 1973).

Thomas, David A. *Christopher Columbus: Master of the Atlantic* (André Deutsch, 1991).

Thompson, John A. F. *The Transformation of Medieval England, 1370–1529* (Longman, 1983).

Townsend, Richard F. *The Aztecs* (Thames and Hudson, 1992).

Tuchman, Barbara W. *A Distant Mirror: The Calamitous 14th Century* (Macmillan, 1979, and Penguin, 1979).

Turner, Geoffrey. *Indians of North America* (Sterling, 1992).

Van Cleave Alexander, Michael. *The First of the Tudors. A Study of Henry VII and His Reign* (Croom Helm, 1981).

Vanes, Jean. *The Port of Bristol in the Sixteenth Century* (Bristol Branch of the Historical Association, 1977).

Vigneras, L. A. New light on the 1497 Cabot voyage to America. *Hispanic American Review*, vol. 36, 1956, pp. 503-506.

Vigneras, L. A. The Cape Breton landfall: 1494 or 1497? Note on a letter from John Day. *Canadian Historical Review*, vol. XXXVIII no. 3, 1957, pp. 219-228.

Weare, G. E. *Cabot's Discovery of North America* (Macqueen, 1897).

Weiditz, Christoph. *Authentic Everyday Dress of the Renaissance* (Dover, 1994).

White, Jon Manchip. *Cortés and the Downfall of the Aztec Empire* (Carroll & Graff, 1971).

Whitfield, Peter. *The Charting of the Oceans: Ten Centuries of Maritime Maps* (The British Library, 1996).

Williamson, James A. *The Cabot Voyages and Bristol Discovery under Henry VII*. Cambridge University Press for the Hakluyt Society, second series no. CXX, 1962.

Wilson, Ian. *The Columbus Myth. Did men of Bristol reach America before Columbus?* (Simon & Schuster, 1992).

Wilson, Ian. *John Cabot and The Matthew, 1497–1997* (Redcliffe Press, 1996).

INDEX

Page numbers in **bold** refer to illustrations

⁂

PICTURE CREDITS